"Immersed in connectedness, compassion, and comedy, Catherine's workbook constructs a home for those of us not fully encompassing the 'young, hyperactive male with attention-deficit/hyperactivity disorder (ADHD)' label. Her warm, informative, and nonjudgmental approach validates and brings real meaning to the experience of neurodivergence in this neurotypically facing world. Catherine, I cannot shout a loud-enough THANK YOU for creating something so many of us have so desperately needed, and not realized!"

—**Jovana Radovic Wood, LMFT,** clinical director and therapist at
the Hallowell Todaro ADHD Center

"This book is the missing piece for most teen girls with ADHD, and clinicians working with teen girls who have ADHD. The amount of information that is oozing from this book and the way that it's written is not only approachable, but relatable and engaging. This is the workbook I wish I had when I was first diagnosed with ADHD, but will now use with all my clients moving forward."

—**Kathryn Feder, LMHC, NCC, ESA,** clinical director and
director of school-based services at the Hallowell Todaro ADHD Center,
and adjunct professor of school counseling at Seattle University

"This workbook is a revelation: an accessible, tender, and engaging read that youth (and their loved ones!) will find instantly helpful. Too often ADHD is misunderstood and overlooked in this population, leading to unnecessary suffering. This book aims to bring it into the light with kindness and a personalized approach."

—**Francesca J. Vash, APNP, FNP-BC,** nurse practitioner in pediatric primary
care at Group Health Cooperative of Southern Wisconsin, and parent of two children
with ADHD

UNDERSTAND YOUR NEURODIVERGENT BRAIN,
MAKE THE MOST OF YOUR STRENGTHS
& BUILD CONFIDENCE TO THRIVE

THE
ADHD WORKBOOK
FOR
TEEN GIRLS

CATHERINE J. MUTTI-DRISCOLL, PHD

Instant Help Books
An Imprint of New Harbinger Publications, Inc.

Publisher's Note

This publication is designed to provide accurate and authoritative information in regard to the subject matter covered. It is sold with the understanding that the publisher is not engaged in rendering psychological, financial, legal, or other professional services. If expert assistance or counseling is needed, the services of a competent professional should be sought.

I would like to dedicate this book to Fran Jeffries and Catherine Driscoll, circa 1993–1998. Without our friendship, the teen years would've been so much more difficult for me. You were the kind of true friend that I now know insulated me from so many ADHD risk factors during my teen years. You were a place to take refuge and be as authentic as I could be at the time. I hope that I have been all these things for you as well. I am very proud of how far we've come.

CONTENTS

FOREWORD

When Catherine Mutti-Driscoll asked me to write a foreword for her new book, I was honored, but I didn't know what I could offer that would be useful to Catherine or the readers and users of this workbook, which, after all, was written not just to be read but also to be used until it looks like an old rag doll that's survived a childhood or two.

As I read through the workbook and thought about what value I might add, my constant response couldn't have been simpler: I kept saying to myself, "Wow! This is great!"

I am adept enough with words to be able to take that simple gut reaction and weave it into a more formal piece of prose—you know, the sort of polished, professional writing that puts on its Sunday best—but I said to myself, "Why do that? Isn't my simple, unguarded response the most useful one?" So I decided to remain in my work clothes and boots and let the words fall where they may.

When you take into account where I am coming from, I can add value just by commenting at all, because I can add the perspective of lived history. I am seventy-three years old, have ADHD myself, and have been treating people of all ages since 1981, the year I first learned about what was then called ADD, and I've written twenty-four books, four of them about what I still call ADD. My entire career and personal life meandered up on the trellis of ADD.

So when I say, "Wow! This is great!" it carries the authority of some forty years of experience as well as thousands of patients treated. I suppose by now I could be considered an *eminence grise.*

Catherine, on the other hand, is an *eminence jeune.* But, boy, oh boy, has she ever packed a ton of knowledge and practical tips into her years, *jeune* or not. I love how she has turned that most difficult of tricks: She has composed a workbook that is both educational and practical but also charming, fun, engaging, and interactive. I urge you to fill in the blanks Catherine has created for you. It will make the book even more useful.

She couldn't have made this workbook as engaging and helpful as it is if she didn't have firsthand, from-the-trenches-of-life experience. That's the best kind of knowledge because it is earned, not just acquired. I can tell that for Catherine this workbook is a labor of love, the love she feels for the people she knows she can help by giving them the knowledge she's worked so hard to acquire. She knows there's not much money to be made in books like this one. But there is a huge intangible profit for both reader and author. The reader's reward you can find on every page of this workbook. And the author's reward, if I may dare say so, is found in the realization of a dream. There was a time, I'll bet, when Catherine lay in bed and went to sleep dreaming of composing this book. But unlike many people who dream of writing a book, Catherine wrote one, and wrote it beautifully.

So what you hold in your hands right now is one person's hard-earned knowledge wrapped in love. This workbook will help anyone who's interested in ADHD, especially its target audience, teen girls.

On behalf of all of us who've already benefited from reading what you've written, Catherine, let me just say, *Thank you!*

—Edward M. Hallowell, MD

INTRODUCTION FOR READERS

Welcome! It's nice to meet you! Per social norms, I should introduce myself. I am Catherine and I was diagnosed with ADHD at age thirty-seven, in 2018. Since then, I have become an ADHD life coach and have begun to learn that ADHD very much runs in my family and shapes my life and relationships in meaningful ways. I have tried to make this book accessible to as many teens with ADHD who do not meet the white young hyperactive male stereotype of ADHD. While I hope that many will relate to the depictions of ADHD showcased in this book, it is important to note that I am very much shaped by my age, race, gender, sexuality, and particular brand of neurodiversity. If you're not familiar with the term *neurodiversity*, it means brain diversity. It is a newer term to describe brains that are not "neurotypical," but are, instead, diverse. People with autism, ADHD, and other mental health conditions are described as *neurodivergent*. This term is meant to help destigmatize brain diversity because differences are often evolutionarily helpful in nature.

To represent the great diversity of ADHD stories, I have created four composite characters that combine the experiences of people I've read about, clients I've seen, and people I've known. These characters are fictional, and do not represent real people. I hope that you will be able to relate to the strengths and/or challenges described in these composite characters. However, four stories would never be enough to represent all the diversity of ADHD because everyone with ADHD is uniquely themselves and therefore what strategies and supports work for them are unique too.

A NOTE ON GENDER

When I use the term "ADHD girls," I mean it very broadly to encompass teens who do not identify with the stereotypically male symptoms of ADHD, who identify as female, and who feel like they wrestle with the gender expectations and challenges frequently placed on girls and women.

HOW TO USE THIS BOOK

I recommend using this book as it works for you. I would be remiss to recommend otherwise, as I'm guessing, with your ADHD brain, that it's important for you to do things your way. My ADHD brain is that way. I must do the task my way or it won't be done. If you are someone who wants to learn more about ADHD and ADHD brains, I recommend starting at the beginning. If you are planning an evaluation or trying to get more support, I recommend intentionally reading the material and completing the activities so that you can share them with a medical provider who can diagnose this condition. Your work can be shown to a provider so that they can more easily understand how your symptoms are showing up for you. This will help ensure that you get the most accurate diagnosis and the most helpful support for you possible.

If you skim the book and don't answer any of the question prompts, I won't be offended. In all honesty, that is my most common way of making a first pass through a workbook. My brain is stimulated by the new information, but then stopping and reflecting can feel too hard at times. I frequently come back later to complete the reflections (well, I *sometimes* do 😄). If you are someone who prefers to reflect by drawing rather than writing, feel free to use the empty space on the pages to draw instead of write, or use a sketchbook to accompany your use of this book. If you like to employ the other common ADHD strategy of collecting books but rarely getting around to reading them, I won't judge you for that either. I assure you that this book will make an excellent coaster or addition to one of the ADHD piles in your room (that is, if you have ADHD piles). I appreciate the good intentions that you bring to reading this book, or the good intention of the person who gave it to you. That intention is all it takes for you to belong here, with us.

CHAPTER 1

LEARNING ABOUT ADHD

You are here. These first two chapters represent the dot on the map that announces *you are here.* Here we are at the intersection of time, four letters, and gender. The journey begins in chapter 1 with an imperfect acronym, ADHD. This acronym has been historically ascribed to males. Now we know it is much broader and bigger than that. *This is where our journey begins.*

What Does ADHD Mean?

The acronym "ADHD" is thrown around a lot, but what does it mean? It stands for attention deficit hyperactivity disorder, the most updated term in the esteemed psychology bible, the *Diagnostic and Statistical Manual of Mental Disorders*, volume 5. Phew, that was a mouthful. Let's read that again. Attention *deficit* hyperactivity *disorder.* My mind catches on the terms "deficit" and "disorder." Ouch. I have a *deficit* and a *disorder*? That sounds bad, right? Even the term "hyperactivity" doesn't sound good, but at least it sounds less negative than "deficit" and "disorder."

If you think that attention deficit hyperactivity disorder is an imperfect title for how our brains work, you are not alone. Many experts agree that the name should be changed. Even though the name sounds negative, I assure you that ADHD is not as scary as it sounds. After I was diagnosed, I finally found the self-understanding and connection I had always been seeking. I found out that an estimated 10 percent of the population have ADHD. I wasn't alone, and neither are you. Ironically, getting this diagnosis and the right support and resources made me feel *less* disordered than I ever had before. There was a name for my particular kind of difference!

Many people start questioning whether they have ADHD (or others around them question it) when a *tipping point* occurs. A tipping point is a time when the demands of our lives are too much for us to manage in a way that seems "normal" or "typical." For some of us, the demands of sitting still in kindergarten reveal our challenges, while others of us struggle when we begin middle school and the expectations for self-management increase. Still others of us face ADHD challenges as we go to high school, attend college, get married, or become parents.

The tricky part of the "tipping point" is that our tipping point must occur at a time when we are able to access knowledge about ADHD, or others around us must know enough about ADHD to suspect that this is the cause of our challenges. If a person has a tipping point but lacks knowledge about what ADHD looks like in their population, or if others around them don't recognize this struggle, that person is unlikely to get diagnosed.

When did you first hear about ADHD? What did you learn?

When did you or others start to wonder whether you had ADHD? When you first heard about ADHD, did you relate to it?

Do you think you had a tipping point? When? Was it recognized by you or others?

What was going on in your life when you started to suspect you had ADHD? Was there a major change in your life at that time?

_____

_____

_____

_____

_____

_____

_____

_____

I'M FEELING BAD ABOUT MY ADHD DIAGNOSIS (OR SUSPECTED DIAGNOSIS)!

Perhaps in part because ADHD sounds scary, many people grieve when they first learn that they have it. Sometimes our family members have grief about our diagnosis too. Other times, it is relieving to have a name that explains why we are struggling, and it gives us hope that we will receive more understanding and support in the future. If you have difficult or complex feelings about your ADHD, journaling can be a great way to process your experiences.

How did you first feel about this idea that you might have ADHD? Did you feel grief, sadness, hope, or relief? Share how you were feeling about your diagnosis when you first received it. How do you feel now? If you would rather draw a picture of the memory that shows how you felt, feel free!

If you don't like saying you have ADHD because it sounds negative, you might prefer a more recent term that celebrates the natural brain diversity that humans have. You can describe yourself as having a "neurodivergent brain" if you like this way of self-identifying better. In case you skipped the introduction (many ADHD brains are prone to doing this! 😄), saying you have a neurodivergent brain means that you have brain diversity, which differs from most brains (or the expected brain). Expected brains are the kind of brains the majority of folks have, and are described as *neurotypical*. The term *neurodivergent* is meant to highlight and celebrate the diversity of brains, which people with ADHD, autism, and other mental health conditions are thought to have. In nature, diversity is normal, natural, and extremely helpful! This term tries to highlight the benefits of different forms of diversity, thereby destigmatizing neurodivergent brains.

Would you rather identify yourself as having ADHD or having a neurodivergent brain? What makes you prefer one over the other?

_____

_____

_____

_____

Are You Inattentive?

Now we will dive into the deeper meaning of ADHD and how it gets diagnosed. Many mental health and health professionals, including therapists, nurses, doctors, psychologists, and psychiatrists, can diagnose ADHD. These professionals look for a history of inattention, hyperactivity, and impulsivity. Let's start with what inattention looks like.

I define *inattention* as difficulty paying attention to the main content of an event. In practice, difficulty paying attention is not as easy to diagnose as it sounds. Even my definition sounds a bit squishy and confusing, doesn't it? I'll explain. For example, when you are out in the world there is typically a reason you are in a particular place. When you attend school, you are supposed to be focusing on that. When hanging out with friends, you are supposed to listen when others talk. When you go to a movie, you are supposed to be watching the movie. If you are having trouble focusing on the main content of a situation, you may be struggling with inattention. I know, I know, the "main content" of a situation can be up for debate. Still, people with ADHD are people who struggle to focus on what they are "supposed to" be focusing on in multiple settings and they do so *significantly more* than people without ADHD.

Inattentive symptoms can show up in different ways. For some, it shows up as being distracted by thoughts and feelings inside of themselves. This looks like spacing out, daydreaming, or ruminating (mulling things over excessively). For others, it can show up as being distracted by things outside of the person, including sounds, other people, our phones, and yes, for some of us, squirrels (this is a common ADHD joke 😄).

Some people don't flag themselves as having ADHD because they notice how they can pay attention well in some areas, which is actually true for many people with ADHD. The flip side of ADHD lack of focus (or inattention) in particular areas is an abundance of focus in other areas. This is called *hyperfocus*. Typically, it is easy for the person with ADHD to focus in areas that are of interest to them and difficult in settings where they aren't as engaged.

To figure out whether inattention is an issue for you, you can notice what, if any, situations feel challenging to pay attention to. Try brainstorming some on the next page. On the flip side, you can also notice when it is easy for you to pay attention. Do you notice any patterns?

EASY TO PAY ATTENTION TO	HARD TO PAY ATTENTION TO

Are you more distracted externally, internally, or some of both? (*External distractions* can include other people, the environment, the scenery, technology, and certain activities. *Internal distractions* can include thoughts and feelings.)

_____

_____

What situations or things tend to distract you the most?

_____

_____

_____

If you think you might be inattentive, what does your inattention look like? Do you space out, daydream, or ruminate at times when you should probably be paying attention?

_____

_____

_____

HELP! CAN'T FOCUS WHEN I NEED TO! WHAT DO I DO?

People with ADHD have *interest-driven nervous systems* (Dodson 2022). This means that we have a much easier time paying attention when we are interested with what is going on in a particular situation. I bet there are a lot of times that you *can* focus when you're interested. Don't forget to give yourself credit for the things you can focus on!

What are some things you are awesome at focusing on?

_____

_____

_____

_____

For the things that are hard to focus on, is there any way you can add a splash of interest? Could you do something interesting *before* the awful boring task, pair the awful boring task with something interesting (e.g., listen to music), or give yourself an interesting reward after the awful boring task? Brainstorm some strategies that might help you focus below:

_____

_____

_____

_____

_____

Do You Have ADHD with the H?

Hyperactivity is defined very much as it sounds—an overabundance of movement, activity, or energy. Hyperactivity is a misunderstood symptom, and that is why it can be hard to identify. I was once in an online meeting with a group of ADHD women and made a joke about how I kept moving around and not sitting still. I was greeted with silence—complete crickets. You may suspect it was my sense of humor, but I don't think that was it...I think it has to do with how hyperactivity is misunderstood in girls and women. Similarly, I have heard many women my age share that they have "ADHD without the *H*."

The *H* is part of my diagnosis, and it looks different than you might think. I am not bouncing off the walls (in fact, I am sometimes extremely sleepy), but I am often fidgeting (twirling my hair), restlessly completing chores, or getting up to go to the bathroom and move my legs. The hyperactive *H* also shows up for some as verbal hyperactivity (talking a lot) or mental hyperactivity, which has been described by some as having a "fast brain" or many thoughts.

The *H* is also misunderstood because people assume that those who are doodling, moving around, or talking a lot are unfocused. In reality, a lot of us have an easier time focusing when we are walking, playing sports, drawing, or fiddling with a fidget. If I am talking to someone and they are moving around a lot, I don't take it personally because I know they are likely working hard to engage with me.

How, if at all, does hyperactivity show up for you? Do you talk a lot, move around a lot, or fidget? Do you have a fast brain with a lot of thoughts? Does moving your body ever help you focus better?

Have you ever been misunderstood due to your hyperactivity symptoms? What was going on at the time? Describe the situation or draw a picture of the memory below.

HELP! I HAVE VERBAL HYPERACTIVITY!

Many girls with ADHD are told they talk and interrupt "too much." If this sounds like you, a quick strategy that can help with this is trying to focus on listening to the other person with an eye toward being able to summarize what they said back to them. This strategy provides a focus for each conversation that can help your ADHD brain know what it should be doing. If I try to focus on and remember what another person says, then I can't just focus on what I'm about to say as I also really have to focus on listening.

How, if at all, might you apply this strategy?

_____

_____

_____

_____

What about this strategy might be helpful for you? What about this strategy might not work for you? Are there any other strategies that you've found work better for you in managing your verbal hyperactivity?

_____

_____

_____

_____

_____

_____

_____

Are You Impulsive?

Impulsivity means acting without thinking or intention. When I used to think of the term "impulsivity," I pictured an angry male who couldn't control his outbursts or aggressive behavior. However, this term can also describe less obvious, everyday behaviors. For example, when I don't follow through on a plan I made earlier because I don't "feel like it" or it no longer sounds good, appealing, or reasonable, I am acting impulsively. When I decide to online shop instead of working on my writing, I am acting impulsively. You may be wondering, *What's the difference between impulsivity and spontaneity?* Good question. Impulsivity takes me away from what is important to me, whereas spontaneity could be a decision that is made quickly but still in accordance with what is meaningful to me. When we are impulsive, we haven't paused even momentarily to consider the meaning or implications of our actions. Another term for this lack of reflection is *autopilot mode.*

Overall, I am a pretty controlled person. However, I have behaved impulsively in my speech, blurting out mean comments or teasing others when I was jealous. I have also behaved impulsively around food, planning to eat healthily but then draining my energy and eating empty calories to cope with my long, overwhelming to-do list. I have shopped online when I was feeling down, even though I wanted to get a better handle on my budget. As you complete the reflections below, consider whether you can relate to any of the examples I've shared.

What internal or external circumstances trigger your more intentional, self-aware, and controlled behavior?

_____

_____

_____

What internal or external circumstances trigger your impulsive, less self-aware, and less controlled behavior?

_____

_____

_____

_____

HELP! I WANT TO BETTER CONTROL MY BEHAVIOR!

If you want to do a behavior less, make it harder to do. If you want to do a behavior more, make it easier to do. For example, if you want to eat less sugar, don't have sugar in the house. If you want to be distracted by your phone less, put it in an alternative location while studying or adjust the settings to work mode. If you want to drink less caffeine, make decaf coffee at home or purchase a decaf at a coffee shop.

What are your strategies for controlling behaviors that get easily out of hand for you? How can you make it harder to do the behavior you don't want to do as often? How could you make it easier to practice alternative behaviors?

_____

_____

_____

_____

_____

_____

ACTIVITY 5

What Is Your ADHD Subtype?

Now that we have reviewed the symptoms that make up the diagnostic criteria for ADHD, we can discuss the three types of ADHD as defined in the current *DSM-5*.

- **ADHD PREDOMINANTLY HYPERACTIVE/IMPULSIVE PRESENTATION.** You may have this type if you mostly struggle with hyperactivity and impulsivity in their various forms. Challenges of this subtype may include physical, verbal, or mental hyperactivity; fidgeting; restlessness; lack of self-control; lack of emotional control; difficulty following stated or unstated rules; and social challenges.

- **ADHD PREDOMINANTLY INATTENTIVE TYPE.** With this subtype, you may be easily bored, forgetful, and have difficulty getting things done. You may also have trouble organizing yourself to get started or follow through on tasks. Finally, you may experience mood and emotional regulation issues as well.

- **ADHD COMBINED PRESENTATION.** If both the above descriptions resonate with you, you may have the combined presentation of ADHD.

As I mentioned, I was not diagnosed with ADHD as a teen, but if I had been, you would have seen my ADHD combined type symptoms showing up as a desire to always be doing something outside the house with my best friend, difficulty relaxing (alone especially), twirling my hair, ruminating on worries, spacing out in group social conversations that I found boring, and challenges with self-discipline around personal care habits and routines. I struggled to organize my stuff, interrupted others more than I would have liked, and experienced mood issues. I hyperfocused on school, obsessed about whether others liked me, and found stress management difficult.

If my past teen self met you at school, what would I see? What would your ADHD look like through the eyes of a peer?

_____

_____

_____

_____

If we met as teens, do you think we would be friends or do you think we would annoy each other, either because we are too similar or because we struggled with similar challenges?

_____

_____

_____

 **HELP!**

I'm Feeling Overloaded with All of This Information!

I know this is a lot of information! To help you synthesize it, I have made a chart of common inattentive, hyperactive, and impulsive symptoms. You'll also find a copy of this chart at the website for this book: http://www.newharbinger.com/52809. You can come back to this chart over time as you gain self-awareness and are better able to notice your behavior and symptoms.

Looking at the list below, which symptoms do you identify with? Circle the ones that most resonate with you. If you are not sure whether you experience some of these symptoms, that is normal. I found that my awareness of my symptoms grew over time, which made me better able to rate my symptoms in surveys and checklists like these. If you are already accessing services for ADHD, you may want to show your provider this chart to communicate about your experiences more easily and where you might need support. If you start to suspect you have the wrong subtype, don't worry. If you have the diagnosis, you can already receive those services and benefits to help your ADHD. A more accurate diagnosis just helps you know which symptoms to work on and get support for in the future.

ADHD Symptoms		
INATTENTIVE	**HYPERACTIVE**	**IMPULSIVE**
Easily bored	Talks a lot	Lack of self-control
Spacey	Moves around a lot	Hasty comments
Daydreamy	Fidgety	Social conflict
Ruminating	Difficulty relaxing	
Distracted by internal or external stimuli	Fast brain	
"Too much" attention in areas of interest		
"Too little" attention in areas that are not of interest		

Based on the above chart, which subtype do you most relate to?

_____

If you have a diagnosis, do you think you have been diagnosed with the correct subtype?

_____

_____

If you are getting ADHD support already, are those supports targeting your symptoms? Which of your symptoms are well addressed and which aren't?

_____

_____

ACTIVITY 6

Overlooked Emotional Aspects of ADHD

At this point, you may still not know whether ADHD is a term that fits you. Perhaps the discussions of inattentiveness, hyperactivity, and impulsivity don't really resonate. Or maybe they resonate a little bit, but not fully. To help you figure out if you belong in this group, I'm going to share common emotional experiences for ADHDers that are often overlooked. Even if you know you have ADHD already, you still may benefit from learning about some of the emotional aspects of ADHD.

COMMON ADHD EXPERIENCE #1: REJECTION SENSITIVITY DYSPHORIA

Rejection sensitivity dysphoria (RSD) represents the experience of having extreme emotional reactions (sometimes experienced as physical pain) to the reality or perception of being rejected or criticized. Many stressful circumstances can trigger an RSD response, even if our feelings of rejection weren't intended by the other person. RSD reactions can even occur when an ADHDer is alone but feels they have not met their own high standards of behavior or productivity. A feeling of failure can be experienced by an ADHDer as a challenging emotional response (Dodson 2022).

COMMON ADHD EXPERIENCE #2: EMOTIONAL HYPERAROUSAL

Emotional hyperarousal describes the nature of the up and down emotions that people with ADHD often experience. People with ADHD often experience higher highs and lower lows; have emotions that change rapidly; and can have trouble relaxing, winding down to sleep, or transitioning from task to task. This intense emotionality can at times be quite overwhelming for the person with ADHD and can also confuse others. Emotional hyperarousal can also make it very easy for a person with ADHD to make harsh, snap judgments about themselves, others, or social situations and experiences.

How, if at all, do you relate to one or both of these two common ADHD emotional experiences, RSD and emotional hyperarousal?

_____

_____

_____

Do you frequently take criticism harshly and have a hard time letting it go? Do you often judge yourself when you aren't able to meet your standards of performance?

_____

_____

_____

Can you reflect on an experience where you felt judged by yourself or someone else? What happened in the situation, and how did you react?

_____

_____

_____

_____

HELP! I FEEL LIKE A FAILURE!

Due to emotional hyperarousal and RSD, people with ADHD often feel like they are failing even if they aren't. If you've ever felt like a failure, I want you to know that you aren't alone in feeling this way. Here are a few strategies to help defuse these intense emotions so you can work with them more skillfully over time.

- **FIRST,** work on calming yourself down. Is there anything you can do to let go and release these emotions? Anything you can do to comfort yourself? Could you take a bath, relax, go for a walk?

- **SECOND,** once you are calm enough to step back from the situation, find a way to reflect on it. You might process the situation by writing or talking it through with a trusted friend, therapist, or coach. Ask yourself: What really happened in the situation? Was it really a failure/rejection or did it just feel like one? Is there any other way to view the situation in a less harsh light?

- **THIRD,** try to separate what you did from who you are. If you made a mistake, recognize that that doesn't mean you *are* a mistake. If you did something "bad," that doesn't mean you *are* bad. See the difference here?

- **FOURTH,** recognize what you can and can't control. Are you blaming yourself for something that is outside of your sphere of influence? For example, as a student, I worked very hard. Even though I did my best, I would feel shame if I received a less than perfect grade. However, even if we work hard, we can't control how someone else perceives the quality of our product. Arguably, we can't control even whether we produce a quality product, we can only show up and do our best. Taking a bad grade personally as a failure doesn't really make sense because it's outside of our control. Looking back, I can see how taking a bad grade personally didn't really make sense since how the teacher assessed the product I created was outside of my control.

Can you think of a time when you've felt like a failure? What was going on in the situation?

_____

_____

_____

_____

_____

When your inner critic labeled you as a failure, do you think that label was fair or do you think the situation was more complicated?

_____

_____

_____

_____

When you felt like a failure, were you blaming yourself for something outside of your control? If you feel the situation was within your control, can you try to zoom out and offer yourself some compassion? No matter what happened, I'm guessing you were doing the very best that you could in that moment. How, if at all, can you appreciate yourself for doing the best you knew how to do at the time?

_____

_____

_____

_____

Getting Support

Some people suspect they have ADHD but choose not to get diagnosed because they don't feel like their ADHD is causing that many challenges, don't trust medical professionals to give them an accurate diagnosis, or don't feel that the time and expense of the process are worth it. All of these reasons for not pursuing a diagnosis are valid and okay. Some teens may also have found ways to get some supports for their challenges without an ADHD diagnosis. For example, people can still access therapy, seek out coaching, or receive school supports without an ADHD diagnosis. Getting supports for these issues even without a diagnosis can still be very helpful.

If you choose to pursue a diagnosis, here are some of the benefits that could exist on the other side. First, you must have an ADHD diagnosis to be able to utilize ADHD medication. Medication helps many peoplefocus better, supporting them in being able to implement helpful behavioral and organizational strategies. Second, you will feel more kinship with other people who have ADHD and can join groups and communities with similar challenges. These ADHD supports may be more likely to be covered by insurance if you have a diagnosis. You may have also an easier time getting school supports for ADHD.

Some people decide to get evaluated for ADHD and they do not receive the diagnosis. This can be disappointing if a person was looking for an explanation and validation of their experience. While I was lucky enough to be validated in my suspicions regarding most of the diagnoses I have been evaluated for, I have known some clients who have not met the diagnostic criteria upon first evaluation. I encourage people to try again if they believe something was missed. Sometimes parents or teachers will fill out forms for students but not really understand what the form is asking or how ADHD shows up, or maybe the teacher hasn't known the student long enough to make an accurate evaluation. You can go back to the same provider with new evidence, or you can find a new one and get a second opinion.

Where are you in the diagnosis process? Are you deciding whether to try, seeking a diagnosis, or trying to organize some resources to get started on the diagnosis process?

What, if any, obstacles are getting in the way of getting the support you need? What kind of support would help you in your next steps to learn about ADHD and manage your challenges?

_____

_____

_____

_____

_____

 # I'M FEELING OVERWHELMED!

If you are overwhelmed by contemplating the process of getting diagnosed or accessing further ADHD supports, you are not alone. When you have ADHD and you choose to get diagnosed or access resources, you have a lot to manage. In many ways, you will be the case manager for yourself and your medical care. This is not easy because many ADHD challenges get in the way of doing this kind of case management. You are not alone if you find this daunting, and if you need to ask for help with organizing all of this, that's nothing to be ashamed of. These multistep projects can be hard for many of us to manage.

If you want to ask for help, but don't know how to (many of us can have trouble with getting started on tasks and social communication challenges), I recommend thinking of one person you could ask for help about this, and use the sample script below if you don't know what to say. You can email, call, or talk in person as you feel comfortable. If it turns out that the person you selected doesn't know much about ADHD or ADHD among your population, try to pick yourself up, dust yourself off, and ask someone else. You'll find a copy of this exercise at the website for this book, http://www.newharbinger .com/52809, so you can easily access it as you seek resources and treatment along your ADHD journey.

Here are some people you might ask for help in doing this case management work. Circle the possible people you might talk to.

★ **YOUR PARENT OR GUARDIAN**

★ **SCHOOL COUNSELOR**

★ **A FRIEND WHO HAS ADHD**

★ **AN ADULT YOU KNOW WHO HAS ADHD**

★ **SPECIAL EDUCATION TEACHER**

★ **YOUR PEDIATRICIAN**

★ **AN ADHD ORGANIZATION, LIKE THE HALLOWELL OR HALLOWELL TODARO ADHD CENTERS, CHADD, OR SIMILAR RESOURCE CENTER**

SAMPLE SCRIPT

Hi! My name is _____. I am trying to (learn about how to get diagnosed with ADHD, get resources for ADHD, understand accommodation options for ADHD, figure out how to pay for ADHD support). I'm not sure what the next steps are in this process and I was wondering if you had any suggestions for who I might contact or what steps I might take next to get this process started. Thank you for your time and help.

Personalize this script to you and modify it as needed. Can you think of someone you might use this script with?

_____

_____

_____

_____

_____

_____

_____

_____

Who could you reach out to for help managing your ADHD? Would you prefer to ask them in person at school, call their office, or write them an email?

_____

_____

_____

_____

Myths and Stigma Persist

Despite generally increasing awareness and knowledge about ADHD, there are still many myths about who can and cannot have ADHD, and whether the ADHD diagnosis even has validity in the first place. Here are some of the common myths that still impact many people's perceptions about ADHD:

ADHD only occurs in young white boys.

Adults grow out of their ADHD.

ADHD is made up.

Smart people cannot have ADHD.

Research shows that people of all backgrounds, ages, genders, and nationalities have ADHD. Many very smart and gifted people have ADHD. However, not all educators, people in our communities, or even people who diagnose ADHD are always up on the latest research. As a result of misinformation and stereotypes, many individuals in non-white and non-male groups are diagnosed less frequently.

There is also growing awareness regarding how ADHD behaviors have been misunderstood and misattributed to character deficits in the past. ADHD symptoms have previously been viewed as evidence that a person is disrespectful, uncaring, or just lazy. Now we know that these behaviors are, in fact, evidence of a person's brain-based challenges, and not intentional bad behavior. For example, a prominent social psychologist, Dr. Devon Price (2021), recently made the bold claim that "laziness does not exist" in his book of the same title. People often assume that ADHD symptoms can be overcome by working harder. Here are a few mistaken assumptions that people make about ADHD behaviors:

ADHD can be overcome with a good dose of willpower.

If people with ADHD tried hard enough, they could focus.

If people with ADHD tried hard enough, they could stop interrupting people.

If people with ADHD tried hard enough, they could control their annoying behaviors.

If people with ADHD tried hard enough, they could get organized.

Have you come across negative beliefs about ADHD symptoms? Where did you come across these beliefs, and what did you think about them at the time?

_____

_____

_____

_____

_____

_____

_____

When you first heard about ADHD, what were your impressions of it? Have you come across people in your life who believe some of the myths mentioned in this activity?

_____

_____

_____

_____

_____

_____

_____

HELP! I'VE BOUGHT INTO NEGATIVE BELIEFS ABOUT ADHD!

If you have previously labeled your own or someone else's ADHD behavior as lazy, crazy, or stupid, you are not alone. We are all products of our environments, and it is very common to take in the negative beliefs of our culture. This is a process known as *internalization*.

If you have internalized negative beliefs about ADHD, try to have compassion for your very human tendency to absorb your environment. It won't happen overnight, but over time, you will learn how to see ADHD behaviors in less negative ways. After getting diagnosed in 2018, I have come to much more deeply accept and understand that my own ADHD behavior is caused by the natural diversity of my neurodivergent brain. Over time, I've become less self-critical when I mess up. Sometimes I can almost even find symptoms like leaving my purse on the roof of my car and driving away to be funny. *Almost funny.*

Which of your ADHD symptoms, mistakes, or behaviors could you try to see in a slightly more compassionate light? (When it comes to self-compassion, even a little bit can go a long way.)

_____

_____

_____

_____

_____

_____

ADHD Strengths

Many people argue that ADHD is not just a deficit or a disorder, but also a gift, a superpower, and a condition that delivers many strengths. ADHD expert Dr. Edward Hallowell (2023) speaks and writes about how ADHD's so-called challenges have positive flip sides. For example, hyperactivity can be reframed as energy, drive, and an ability to act. Impulsivity overlaps with admirable qualities such as excitement and spontaneity. While ADHDers may have trouble focusing when bored, we tend to be passionately engaged and motivated when interested.

In fact, Dr. Hallowell and his colleague, Dr. Ratey, have proposed a new name for ADHD, variable attention stimulus trait (VAST; 2021). This much more positive-sounding name highlights that our attention varies based on our interest levels and also depends on how well our environment is set up to support our needs. These doctors point out that when we are interested and well-supported, our attention can truly be vast.

Researchers are also learning more about the strengths that people with ADHD often have. For example, people with ADHD often have exceptional strengths in creativity, generating ideas, making connections between ideas, thinking outside of the box, empathy, kindness, and humor.

Which ADHD strengths do you see in yourself?

_____

_____

Can you think of a time when you were able to use one or more of your strengths? What was that experience like?

_____

_____

_____

_____

HELP! I DON'T THINK I HAVE ANY STRENGTHS!

If you feel like your challenges out number your strengths, you're not alone in that feeling. Or if you have fallen into the common trap of not noticing your strengths because you are so focused on fixing your challenges, you're not alone in that either. Many people with ADHD are prone to *perfectionism*, a belief that makes it seem that if we are not perfect in all things, we are bad. Unfortunately, perfectionism is unrealistic and can therefore pose challenges. In expecting ourselves to be perfect and without flaws, we are chasing an unrealistic and unattainable ideal. To support good mental health for ourselves, the goal is to find ways of accepting and managing our challenges while celebrating and leading with our strengths.

What ADHD challenges can you work on accepting more in the future?

_____

_____

_____

_____

_____

What ADHD strengths can you work on recognizing and celebrating in the future?

_____

_____

_____

_____

_____

Chapter Summary

AN ADHD-FRIENDLY STRATEGY THAT OFTEN HELPS ME is when the author summarizes the main points via a bulleted list at the end of the chapter. If an author hasn't done it for you, it can be a helpful exercise to do yourself when you are reading something that you want to retain. You can even take notes as you go so you don't have to look the entire chapter over again.

Content Summary

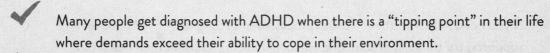

✔ Many people get diagnosed with ADHD when there is a "tipping point" in their life where demands exceed their ability to cope in their environment.

✔ There are three ADHD subtypes listed in the current *DSM-5*: ADHD hyperactive-impulsive type, ADHD predominantly inattentive type, and ADHD combined type.

✔ ADHD is diagnosed by observing the criteria of inattention, hyperactivity, and impulsivity in a person's behavior.

✔ People with ADHD have *interest-driven nervous systems* and can often hyperfocus when interested in something but struggle to pay attention when not interested.

✔ Rejection sensitivity dysphoria and emotional hyperarousal are common emotional experiences for people with ADHD.

✔ ADHD is caused by brain-based challenges, not by a failure of character or lack of willpower.

✔ Even though all groups are not diagnosed at the same rates, research shows that people of all backgrounds, ages, genders, and nationalities have ADHD. Many very smart and gifted people have ADHD.

STRATEGY SUMMARY

★ If you don't like using the term "ADHD," you can say you have a "neurodivergent brain" instead.

★ Adding things that interest you before, during, or after a task can boost your focus.

★ If you want to do a behavior less, make it harder to do. If you want to do a behavior more, make it easier to do.

★ If you need help with the multistep processes of getting diagnosed or accessing supports, try thinking of someone you could ask for help and then reach out.

★ To manage verbal hyperactivity, focus on listening to what the other person is saying so well that you could summarize it back to them.

★ Carefully manage any common feelings of failure by getting calm, reviewing the situation, separating your behavior from your identity, and not blaming yourself for things you cannot control.

★ All of these possible strategies for managing your ADHD take practice, so try to have compassion for yourself along the way.

CHAPTER 2

ADHD AND GENDER

So far, we have covered quite a bit of helpful information about everyone's favorite imperfect acronym, ADHD. Now we are going to dive into how ADHD intersects with gender and how it often can show up for individuals who are missed for a diagnosis. This will be helpful information for you to have no matter if you are seeking a diagnosis or if you already have one and are wanting to learn how to best manage your ADHD.

Historically Missed Girls

The fact that you are here learning about ADHD is not just a big win for your self-knowledge personally. It also represents huge progress for our knowledge about ADHD in girls and in women generally. Many women in my generation had the experience of learning about their ADHD later in life. Some articles call my generation of women with ADHD "the missed generation."

You may be asking, and I certainly have asked many times, why women like me were missed for the diagnosis and why some girls are still missed today. A big part of why girls were missed for the diagnosis is that their inattentive, hyperactive, and impulsive symptoms didn't show up in the same way that these symptoms showed up in boys (McCabe 2021), especially hyperactive and impulsive boys who were easy for people to spot and diagnosticians to identify. In fact, statistics show that girls are missed for the diagnosis three to four times more frequently than their hyperactive male peers (McCabe 2016). Other groups, such as boys with predominantly inattentive ADHD, people of color, and gifted individuals, are also often frequently missed for an ADHD diagnosis. These populations often present symptoms that are missed, or the symptoms come in a package that looks so unlike the ADHD stereotype that it isn't noticed.

MISSED SYMPTOMS VS. NOTICED SYMPTOMS

In the following chart, I have brainstormed a list of common symptoms of ADHD. Some of them are flagged as ADHD more often than others. Can you identify which of these symptoms are more likely to be noticed and which are more often missed? Make a check mark to indicate which of the symptoms below you would guess are more likely to be noticed or missed in diverse teens.

	MISSED	NOTICED
Annoys, teases, and insults others		
Physically aggressive		
Self-critical		
Low self-esteem		
Interrupts people		
Spaces out frequently		
Anxiety or depression		
Argues with adults		
Behavior issues at school		

Here are the answers. How did you do?

	MISSED	NOTICED
Annoys, teases, and insults others		✔
Physically aggressive		✔
Self-critical	✔	
Low self-esteem	✔	
Interrupts people		✔
Spaces out frequently	✔	
Anxiety or depression	✔	
Argues with adults		✔
Behavior issues at school		✔

Look at the chart above and note the symptoms that you have. Do you have more commonly missed symptoms or identified symptoms?

_____

_____

_____

_____

HELP! I THINK I'VE BEEN MISSED OR AM LIKELY TO BE MISSED!

If you suspect that your road to accessing a diagnosis and services may be harder if you have missed symptoms or are in a group that is often not diagnosed with ADHD, you're likely correct. If this is your situation, here's what you can do about it.

- Prepare for a diagnostic appointment by reflecting on your challenges and how they might reveal an ADHD diagnosis. Feel free to bring your notes and the work you've done in this book along to your appointment if needed! If this kind of preparation sounds daunting, can you reach out to someone for help?

- Do you know anyone who is knowledgeable about ADHD who you could talk through your ideas about your symptoms with? As an ADHD coach, I help people talk through their challenges and prepare to seek a diagnosis or accommodations. If you can afford it, you might think of working with an ADHD coach to prepare your ideas about why you think an ADHD diagnosis might fit for you.

- Finally, are there any books, podcasts, or YouTube videos that might help you reflect on your experiences? That can be a great way to prepare to advocate for yourself and help you learn how to describe how you think ADHD is showing up for you.

Which of these strategies would be the most accessible or comfortable for you?

_____

_____

_____

_____

_____

ADHD, Gender Identity, and Gender Expectations

When I was growing up, it felt like there were two gender checkboxes. While there was some knowledge about differing sexualities back in the 1990s, it was rarely questioned that a person would identify with the gender they were assigned at birth, based on the genitalia they exhibited. Now we have learned that a person who identifies as a female and was born with a vagina is known as *cisgender*. I am heartened that there are now more options for how people relate to their physical sex characteristics, gender identity, and general social expectations related to gender.

Even though we have made a lot of progress in dismantling gender assumptions and providing increased options for people to express themselves and their gender identity, society still transmits powerful messages about how women and men should act. Men are expected to act in "masculine" ways and women are expected to act in "feminine" ways. We have learned that these common gender expectations are cultural and not natural because gender expectations and behavior vary from society to society. However, the messages we receive about how women and men *should* act can be quite powerful. We can also experience a variety of negative consequences for not living up to these ideals or acting in a gender-nonconforming way.

Many of us with ADHD often find that the male and female checkboxes don't completely fit. Historically, many women with ADHD were labeled "tomboys" or struggled with "feminine" abilities such as organization and social tasks that women were expected to be good at. Not surprisingly, it is more common for people with ADHD to question their gender identity.

What are the messages that you have received about how girls and boys should act, what boys and girls should be good at, and what interests boys and girls should have?

What gender were you assigned at birth based on your physical characteristics? Do you identify with the traits frequently ascribed to your gender? How so or how not? What pronouns do you use to show people how you identify gender-wise (e.g., she/her, he/him, they/them)?

_____

_____

_____

_____

When people accused me of being unfeminine growing up, I felt very hurt. These observations made me feel ashamed and triggered my intense sensitivity. How do you feel about being perceived as feminine? Is it something you are striving for, something that isn't very important to you, or something that doesn't fit at all?

_____

_____

_____

If being perceived as feminine is something that is important to you, what benefits do you expect you would get from acting more feminine?

_____

_____

_____

_____

HELP! I WANT TO USE THEY/THEM PRONOUNS BUT IT FEELS LIKE TOO MUCH WORK FOR MY ADHD!

For some of us, we may feel like the gender pronouns we are assumed to have don't fit but it is overwhelming to think about sharing this with everyone all the time. We may feel overwhelmed by the need to explain our gender identity to many people, especially if those people are older and might not understand. Since we already feel "different" because of our ADHD, feeling "different" because of our gender pronouns may be hard for us.

If you want to use they/them pronouns but feel overwhelmed by sharing this information or explaining your choice, is there someone who is supportive who could help you spread the initial word so you don't have to tell everyone? If people already know, you may not have to feel like you have to explain as much.

If you don't want to have to explain, but you feel like some people might ask, it can be helpful to develop a one-liner explanation that doesn't invite further conversation. You could say, "I use they/them pronouns because I didn't feel like the stereotypes of girls or boys fit me." Most people will not follow up, but in the off chance someone asks about it, you could repeat, "I didn't feel like the male and female gender roles fit." If the person wants to keep questioning you and you don't want to talk further, you can excuse yourself and walk away.

What pronouns do you currently identify with?

Do you find that communicating about your gender identity is easy for you, challenging, or somewhere in between? What makes this communication easy or hard?

_____

_____

_____

_____

_____

_____

How, if at all, does your ADHD get in the way of being able to consistently communicate about your gender identity preferences?

_____

_____

_____

_____

_____

_____

Changing Bodies and Hormones

If you are finding the teen years to be challenging, you're not alone. You're also not doing it wrong—research has shown that this is a tough time for girls with and without ADHD. Movies, TV shows, and social media often show unrealistic and unattainable examples of life during the teen years.

The teen years usher in a lot of physical changes as our bodies become more adult, and for many of us with ADHD this change can be hard and destabilizing. For some ADHD brains, this is exciting and our brains love the novelty of new clothes, bras, and becoming a woman! For others, it's overwhelming and we wish things would stay the same. For me, I resisted change. I didn't want to go bra shopping, I just wanted life to stay simple. However, when I was teased for having a "monstrous chest" at soccer practice by my male coach (my unsupported new breasts were flopping around more than those of other girls), I had to accept that I was growing up and if I didn't want to attract this kind of attention in the future, I needed to conform and get some sports bras.

You will also experience changes internally. For many girls with ADHD, your menstrual cycle hormones may impact your physical and mental health more than for neurotypical peers. Many neurodiverse girls and women experience more extreme premenstrual symptoms than others, to the point that some are diagnosed with premenstrual dysphoric disorder, or PMDD. If you notice challenging shifts in mood, energy, and cognitive function before you get your period, you might check with your doctor about PMDD. Some girls and women report that their medication doesn't work as well during the PMS phase of their cycle and so they need to come up with some other strategies for managing their moods, motivation, and ability to get things done.

Not only are our bodies changing, but people may also be treating us differently and expecting us to present ourselves differently. Many girls are expected to wear bras, shave their legs, and conform to beauty ideals of thinness. Girls may also be expected to engage in complex beauty routines around makeup and clothes that make them look attractive or sexy to others. Girls often experience challenges related to eating disorders or body self-perception when they have ADHD. If you experience challenges related to body image or food, you may want to work on this area with a trusted therapist, nutritionist, or pediatrician.

Some of us have trouble connecting with our bodies, lacking a sense of body awareness. We might prefer to hang out "in our heads" and learn new things, hear or read about new ideas, or do creative projects. For some of us, this makes it hard to want to pay attention to or take care of our bodies. On the flip side, others of us can enjoy putting makeup on, dressing up, and decorating our bodies, etc. Some find clothes, makeup, and beauty routines super interesting or calming!

What is your relationship to your body like? Do you enjoy taking care of your body or do you find it a nuisance or somewhere in between?

_____

_____

_____

_____

How do you feel about the changes your body is going through? Are you excited to look more like an adult? Does your changing body require new or different levels of maintenance than it used to? Are these routines easy or hard for you? Do you generally opt in or out of these routines?

_____

_____

_____

_____

_____

HELP! I THINK I MIGHT HAVE PMDD!

If you think you might have more extreme ADHD symptoms and challenges during the week before your period, I recommend you talk to your doctor about options that could support you during your cyclical hormonal changes. Your doctor will likely ask you what symptoms you are facing, so it can be good to keep a log of your symptoms and your cycle. You can do this in an app on your phone or use tally marks to track your symptoms in a chart like the one below. You might record some examples of what these symptoms generally look like so you can also share that with your doctor. You'll also find a copy of this chart at the website for this book: http://www.newharbinger.com/52809. You can come back to this chart over time as you gain self-awareness and are better able to notice your behavior and symptoms.

TRACKING SYMPTOMS OF PREMENSTRUAL DYSPHORIC DISORDER (PMDD)						
	PHYSICAL ISSUES (headache, fatigue, cramps, etc.)	ANXIETY	DEPRESSION	DISTRACTIBILITY	IRRITABILITY	IMPULSIVITY
Week 1						
Week 2						
Week 3						
Week 4						

As you reflect on your symptoms over the course of the month—does anything stick out to you? How do you think your hormonal changes might impact your mood and ADHD symptoms?

_____

_____

_____

_____

_____

_____

_____

_____

Increasing Academic Demands

During the teen years, academic challenges ratchet up, demanding more self-control, organization, focus, and motivation. Many girls with ADHD are very smart—some even qualify as gifted—but they may lag behind academically due to the increased organizational demands. This change in demands causes some girls to try harder, becoming hypervigilant and obsessive about keeping up with others. Other girls may become discouraged from trying as they find that their efforts stop yielding the desired results. Either way, these challenges can greatly impact your mental health and confidence.

Along the way, girls may face academic challenges over and above their ADHD, such as discovering they have a learning disability as well. Common learning disabilities are dyscalculia (math), dysgraphia (writing), and dyslexia (reading). If you are concerned that you might be facing an additional learning disability, you can inquire at your school about what assessment and services they might provide. You also might seek out neuropsychological testing to provide you with insight into any potential learning issues.

How, if at all, have you noticed academic demands shifting for you? What parts of your school experience are more challenging? Have any parts of it become more enjoyable, interesting, or easier?

When you face challenges at school, are you more likely to feel discouraged and give up or become obsessed with school and overwork?

How, if at all, are ADHD symptoms impacting you at school? Do you think you might have a learning issue in addition to ADHD? Are you getting any support at school for your challenges? Is this something you might want to investigate in the future?

HELP! I THINK I NEED ACCOMMODATIONS!

Even if you have a diagnosis already, there are extra steps involved in getting accommodations at school. The best place to start for you (and/or your parent/guardian if they can help) is talking to a school staff member who works in the special education department or the school counseling office. Often these staff will know who you should talk to about your challenges and can share options for getting support. If you aren't sure what to ask for, here is a list of common accommodations for people with ADHD. Circle the ones that you think might be helpful and feel free to take this book with you when you have a conversation with a school staff member.

- ★ EXTRA TIME ON TESTS
- ★ ALTERNATIVE TESTING LOCATIONS
- ★ BREAKS TO MOVE AROUND

- ★ EXTENDED OR FLEXIBLE DEADLINES
- ★ SPECIAL SEATING ARRANGEMENTS
- ★ ASSIGNMENT INSTRUCTIONS PROVIDED ORALLY AND IN WRITING

Which of these accommodations would be most helpful for you?

_____

_____

_____

_____

Can you think of any other supports that could be helpful?

_____

_____

_____

_____

Changing Social Relationships

In addition to a changing body and changing academic demands, you will likely also experience changing social dynamics. There are generally three types of social experiences for girls with ADHD (one or more may apply to you, and it may depend on the social setting):

- Some girls struggle when social dynamics become more complex and oriented toward popularity and larger groups in high school.

- Other girls are adept at figuring out the new social rules and enacting them to gain social approval and attention. These girls are great at socializing in the ways that the dominant culture rewards and praises.

- Still other girls can cultivate one or two "best friends" to help them navigate the teen years.

Starting in middle school and high school, female relationships frequently take on a *Mean Girls*-type of quality. Girls who have difficulty understanding social relationships (I'm raising my hand right now) could benefit from watching the 2004 *Mean Girls* movie and learning about the power dynamics that often occur in female relationships in our society. For me, I now look back and realize that not only did I struggle to understand social dynamics during the teen years, but I also struggled with focus in a lot of large social situations. I had a limited social battery and could only enjoy company with people I had a deep connection with for an hour and a half to two hours. I also had a limited set of interests and found it hard to engage with small talk, pop culture, and the like.

How have changing social demands impacted you? Have you been able to read and navigate them easily? Do you find new kinds of group gatherings to be interesting and stimulating?

_____

_____

_____

_____

On the flip side, have you found yourself confused and unsatisfied with the new ways that people relate to each other in middle school and high school? Do you feel you've been left behind? Do you feel you socialize differently than others, possibly in a "nonideal" way?

_____

_____

_____

_____

I HAVE A SHORT SOCIAL BATTERY!

If you have a short social battery, you are definitely *not alone*. While there is no quick fix, here are a few ideas for improving your social experiences and hopefully boosting your social battery life at least a bit.

- **IS THERE ANYTHING YOU CAN DO WITH YOUR HANDS DURING THE GATHERING?** For example, can you use a fidget (Speks magnets are my favorite), draw or doodle, use sticker art, or knit?

- **CAN YOU WORK IN ANY MOVEMENT OR BRAIN BREAKS TO REGROUP?** For example, can you walk to the restroom, get up and refill your snacks, or pop outside for a quick phone break/fresh air?

- **CAN YOU SUGGEST AN INTERESTING ACTIVITY TO THE GROUP?** Some of us focus better in social situations when playing a game we like because it helps us stay engaged in our environment by providing structure and interest. Other party activities that might help you engage include dancing, karaoke, or watching a movie.

Can you think of any other strategies you could use to boost your social battery stamina? If so, what are they?

_____

_____

_____

_____

_____

Meet Other ADHDers

ADHD can look very different for each individual depending on their personal characteristics and experiences. To help you see this variability, and hopefully learn about teens who are similar to you, I'd like you to meet four characters who will travel alongside us throughout the rest of the book. Like you, they will learn key skills, mindsets, and strategies to help them along their way. These characters are based on many people with ADHD whom I have known, worked with, and read about.

✳ JASMINE, AGE 14, COMBINED TYPE, SHE/HER, HETEROSEXUAL

Jasmine is very empathetic and a deeply feeling person. She cares passionately about justice and fair treatment. Jasmine is Black and when she sought help for her depression and anxiety, she couldn't find any therapists who looked like her. She wants to become a therapist someday so that she can support other Black girls. Jasmine loves to write and spends a lot of her time journaling. However, having recently started high school, she is struggling academically and isn't sure she will ever make it to college. People have always told her she is smart and insightful, but that hasn't seemed to translate to good grades in high school. At school, she struggles with being disorganized, following instructions, getting started, completing multistep projects, and doing well in math and science.

* AVERY, AGE 16, COMBINED TYPE, SHE/THEY (GENDER QUESTIONING), HETEROSEXUAL

Avery can only focus when she is moving, like when she is on the soccer field. During class, it is hard to focus, and Avery is always called out for jiggling her leg, doodling, getting up to go to the water fountain "too often," or talking to the person next to her. Avery meets very few of the gender expectations for women, lacking the interest or organizational ability to apply makeup, wear dresses, or flirt. Avery has considered using they/them pronouns because she feels very unfeminine, but it seems like such a process to tell everyone what to call her and constantly correct them. When she needs to explain her gender, she often becomes overwhelmed and clams up. Plus, she likes boys and it's already hard enough for them to see her in an attractive way when she is dominating them on the soccer field. She worries that she might scare off boys if she comes out as genderqueer. Would they not know whom she liked?

* ASHA, AGE 18, PREDOMINANTLY INATTENTIVE TYPE, SHE/HER, LESBIAN

Asha really wants to meet her parents' expectations and make them proud. The trouble is that she is always screwing up—getting parking tickets, losing her phone, showing up late to family gatherings, and finding embarrassing typos in her work. The harder she tries to be a good student, the more of a struggle staying organized, remembering things, and controlling her emotions seem to become. She hasn't told anyone yet, but Asha is pretty sure that she likes girls. To avoid thinking about this, and hide it from herself and others, Asha just works harder on her homework and getting into a good college.

✱ ISABELLA, AGE 17, HYPERACTIVE-IMPULSIVE TYPE, SHE/HER, ASEXUAL/BISEXUAL

Isabella is always in the spotlight, drawing others to her. She is beautiful and succeeds with everything that involves projecting a successful, charismatic, aesthetically pleasing, and charming image. Isabella shines when she is singing, dancing, going to parties, and acting in plays. She has found wonderful outlets for her energy, most of the time. However, people make a lot of assumptions about what a popular and charismatic girl should be like and want. They assume Isabella wants attention, sexual and otherwise. Isabella isn't that interested in romance and sex, and tends to be more drawn to romantic partners, regardless of gender, whom she connects with. She isn't even sure if she is attracted to people in the way most people are or seem to want her to be. She doesn't really care to explore it too much, though, because she is focused on her singing and acting goals at the moment.

What similarities do you have with the girls you've just met? What differences? Are there one or two characters whom you relate to most?

_____

_____

_____

_____

_____

_____

_____

_____

 HELP!

HELP! I HAVE TROUBLE FOCUSING ON READING THIS BOOK!

If you ever have trouble focusing while reading, you're not alone. This is very common for a lot of folks with ADHD, even those who do not have a co-occurring learning disability. If you need to take breaks, or skim or skip parts of the book, that is okay. However, if you really do want to feel engaged in the book you're reading and not miss anything, you can try a few strategies to boost your focus.

* Read the book out loud to yourself to minimize distractions.

* Highlight or underline ideas that are interesting to you or are similar to your experience.

* Write notes in the margins about ideas you find interesting.

* If available, try listening to some or all of the book in audiobook format or invest in an app that can read ebooks to you.

Which of these strategies have you already tried to boost your focus when reading? Which might you want to try in the future?

_____

_____

_____

_____

_____

_____

_____

CHAPTER SUMMARY

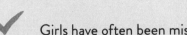

CONTENT SUMMARY

 Girls have often been missed for the ADHD diagnosis because their symptoms show up in different ways than their hyperactive-impulsive male peers.

 Many girls with ADHD struggle with meeting feminine gender expectations and are also more likely to question their gender identity than other girls.

Some girls with ADHD face challenges during the teen years due to their changing bodies, hormonal fluctuations, academic demands, and the increasing complexity of social situations.

STRATEGY SUMMARY

 If you are in a group who is not often diagnosed or have numerous, often-missed symptoms, consider preparing to describe the specific ADHD challenges you see in your life before the diagnostic appointment.

 If relevant, get to know how your menstrual cycle impacts your ADHD symptoms so you can advocate for yourself with your doctor.

 Keep an eye out for body image and disordered eating issues so you can get support if needed (these issues are common in ADHD girls).

 Try using movement and brain breaks if you want to increase your social battery.

 Consider getting help at school with ADHD accommodations and ask school staff about assessments for a possible learning disorder, if suspected.

 If you have trouble focusing on reading, try the following strategies: highlighting or underlining interesting ideas, reading out loud to yourself, writing notes to yourself in the margins, or listening to audiobooks if available.

CHAPTER 3

LEARNING ABOUT YOUR BRAIN

We are beginning a new chapter, so I am returning to the journey metaphor. We started by learning "where we are" by exploring the history of ADHD, the history of ADHD in girls, and learning about the ADHD diagnosis and symptoms to gain a better understanding of our personal history. Now, we need two things for the journey ahead: 1) knowledge about our own unique brain (the components of the vehicle we're driving on the journey) and 2) self-knowledge of who we are and what's important to us (this is what guides us, the map that can show us which direction to go in). This chapter will help you learn about your specific brain—its challenges and its strengths. Learning about our brain is not easy. It requires that we once again accept that we are not perfect (that we have brain-based challenges) while at the same time recognizing what we're good at. It may be hard to hold both our strengths and challenges at the same time, but two things can be, and often are, true at once!

Here are some other things I want you to remember (yes, I am reminding myself too):

- **YOU'RE PERFECT AS YOU ARE,** you are doing this right, and you are not alone.

- **YOU HAVE TIME TO LEARN WHAT YOU NEED TO LEARN,** work on what you need to work on, and figure out what you're here to do.

- **THE ADHD JOURNEY IS LIFELONG.** The activities of understanding our brains and ourselves are also lifelong. But that's okay. We have all that we need, right now in this very moment, even before reading anything further.

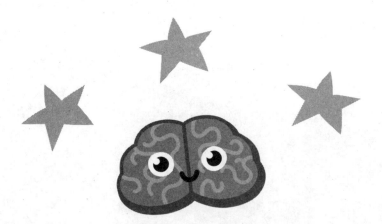

Learning About Your Brain by Looking at Your Behavior

As you'll recall from chapter 1, many people mistakenly believe that our ADHD behavior reveals our moral character—whether we're lazy, stupid, careless, disrespectful, and so on. In reality, our behavior actually reveals our brain's strengths and challenges. Our behavior shows our particular set of *executive function skills*. We will shorten this term to "EF skills" for ease. These skills (or challenges) are controlled by the brain's makeup and development, and not by our individual willpower. We can shape our skills and our brains to some degree, but a big part of our brain's skills and how they function are hardwired, and we are simply made that way. Just like with our ADHD in general, our best bet is to leverage our EF strengths and find ways to manage our challenges.

There are two types of executive functions, those that require thinking (cognition) and those that require doing (behavior). What I didn't understand for many years is that being able to think about something or understand a concept is not the same as being able to do it. These are, in fact, different executive functions. The executive function skills related to action and behavior are sustained attention, response inhibition, task initiation, emotional control, goal-directed persistence, and flexibility. Thinking executive functions including planning/prioritization, working memory, time management, organization, and metacognition (Guare, Dawson, and Guare 2013).

If you don't know what some of these terms mean, don't worry. We will go over all of that in this section so you can learn about your executive function strengths and challenges. Everyone with ADHD has unique EF challenges and strengths. Because of the uniqueness of each person's EF skills, their behavior may look very different from that of family members or friends who have ADHD.

Before we go any further, do you suspect thinking tasks or doing tasks are easier for you?

_____

_____

Some people with ADHD jump into tasks without planning or get stuck in the planning. Can you describe a time when you didn't plan enough? Can you describe a time when you made a plan but couldn't move to action? Which of the above scenarios is more likely to happen to you?

_____

_____

_____

_____

 # I HAVE TROUBLE WITH PLANNING!

Many of us either jump into things without planning or get stuck planning too much and don't do anything. Here are a few quick tips for both sets of challenges.

THE NON-PLANNER

For those of us who dive into tasks with both feet, I recommend trying to make planning feel more active and collaborative. For example, you can plan with a friend, a therapist, or an ADHD coach. You can also plan well in advance of a task so that you don't have to add that mental work at the beginning of the task, which may annoy you, slow you down, or dilute your focus.

THE PLANNING TOO MUCH PLANNER

If you get stuck in the planning phase, try giving yourself a time limit, or limit yourself to how many options you'll research, such as two. You might also consider finding some support for the "doing" part of things. Can you find a person to sit with you while you do the task? This is known as an *accountability buddy*. You can also work with an ADHD coach, who can hold you accountable for getting things done and help you when you get stuck.

As you scan these strategies, which ones do you think might work best for you? What makes you think so?

_____

_____

_____

_____

_____

Which ones do you suspect wouldn't work for you? What makes you suspect that?

_____

_____

_____

_____

_____

Sustained Attention and Response Inhibition

Now that we're discussing how our brains have skills related to thinking and doing, we will start with the EF skills that involve doing. You've already learned two of them when you learned about inattention and impulsivity in the ADHD diagnostic criteria! 😊 Just in case you need a refresher, here are some helpful definitions:

- **INATTENTION** = lack of sustained attention (e.g., struggle with being able to focus despite feeling bored or tired)

- **IMPULSIVITY** = challenge with response inhibition (e.g., struggle with the ability to pause before acting to make sure your actions are intentional, that is, in line with your goals)

Do you remember whether sustained attention (inattention) and response inhibition (impulsivity) were issues for you? Even if you don't recall your earlier reflections on these skills, taking the quizzes below will helpfully aid you in expanding your knowledge of these key EF skills!

SUSTAINED ATTENTION QUIZ (CIRCLE TRUE OR FALSE)

I am often bored.	**TRUE**	**FALSE**
I perform well when interested but struggle to engage when the content isn't interesting to me.	**TRUE**	**FALSE**
I avoid tasks that might be boring, tedious, or difficult.	**TRUE**	**FALSE**
I feel sleepy, restless, or spaced out when teachers, friends, or parents are talking about topics that don't interest me.	**TRUE**	**FALSE**

How many statements did you circle as true? The higher the number, the more likely sustained attention is an issue for you. How many statements did you circle as false? The higher the number, the more likely that sustained attention is a strength for you.

RESPONSE INHIBITION QUIZ (CIRCLE TRUE OR FALSE)

I set goals for doing healthy behaviors but then don't follow through later when tired, overwhelmed, or unmotivated. **TRUE   FALSE**

I speak before thinking. **TRUE   FALSE**

I have a hard time slowing down before I act. I then regret my actions later. **TRUE   FALSE**

I often interrupt others. **TRUE   FALSE**

How many statements did you circle as true? The higher the number, the more likely response inhibition is an issue for you. How many statements did you circle as false? The higher the number, the more likely that response inhibition is a strength for you.

Record your results below.

	STRENGTH	CHALLENGE
Sustained Attention		
Response Inhibition		

I FOCUS TOO MUCH!

For some of us, our sustained attention and our response inhibition impact each other. We start hyperfocusing on something and then we can't stop. However, if we have trouble with response inhibition, we may not be able to stop whatever we're hyperfocusing on. We can keep going and going and going on a task, but may eventually come up for air, and feel depleted and exhausted. This can impact our self-control to manage our relationships, food choices, healthy habits, and so on once we emerge from a draining bout of lengthy hyperfocus.

To counter this challenge, I recommend taking regular breaks from your hyperfocus task (you'll have to experiment with how often the breaks are needed so they don't interrupt your flow. Many people use the *pomodoro method* where they work on a singular task for 25 minutes and then take a 5-minute break. During your breaks, it can help to do some movement or relaxing and easy self-care tasks. These kinds of breaks can support your energy, focus, and help you check in on how you're doing.

What activities are most likely to cause hyperfocus for you? Do you find that hyperfocus can drain your energy? What kind of breaks might help you manage that energy?

_____

_____

_____

_____

_____

Task Initiation

Do you have a hard time getting started on tasks? Are some tasks harder to initiate than others? If so, your brain may have an issue with task initiation. Some of us struggle to get started while others are always ready to launch into action. Most of us struggle with getting started in some areas of our lives—especially on tasks that are boring, tedious, difficult, or stressful, due to our interest-driven nervous systems. As you go through this workbook, keep an eye out for tasks that are easy for you to start and tasks that are difficult to start. Ask yourself: What are the characteristics of the tasks that are easy to start and those that are difficult to start? Knowing what is easy for you to accomplish versus what needs some extra boosts can be really helpful in troubleshooting any task initiation challenges you might run into. In the case studies below, Isabella is good at initiating particular tasks but not others. She also tends to use her task initiation strength too much and can neglect rest and self-care. In contrast, Jasmine has difficulty starting tasks that are not super interesting to her. For Jasmine, task initiation is a common area of challenge.

Isabella is always doing things. Others are often impressed at her energy and how she maintains a full calendar of social activities alongside pursuing her interests in music, acting, and singing classes. Isabella finds that she is very motivated while starting tasks in her interest areas, but struggles to initiate other tasks on her own, especially homework. As a result, she keeps signing up for things, and practicing and studying with others as much as possible. Every once in a while she feels tired, but her energy picks back up quickly, and so she just keeps chugging along as soon as she can. Usually, if she keeps moving, her energy eventually picks up.

Jasmine loves to journal and to come up with ideas to write about. It's easy to get started on writing when she can do it her way—brainstorming ideas, freewriting, being creative. But when asked to write an outline for her English class, Jasmine gets massively stuck. Where should she start? She has no idea how to do this. The more stressed Jasmine becomes, the harder it is to get started. Jasmine decides to take a break and watch YouTube, thinking maybe she'll feel like starting later. All of a sudden, six hours have disappeared and the paper has not been started.

In these case studies, do you relate more to Jasmine or Isabella? Do you think task initiation is a strength or challenge for you, or does it depend greatly on the task or setting?

_____

_____

_____

_____

_____

_____

HOW DO I START TASKS I DON'T LIKE?

A common strategy for working with task initiation challenges is to *pair* the task with something else to make it more pleasant. First, identify a task that is hard to start and then brainstorm what could make it more pleasant. Could you do something *before* the task to boost your energy and motivation? Could you tweak something *during* the task? Could you reward yourself *after* the task?

BOOST BEFORE	TWEAK DURING	REWARD AFTER
Make environment more comfortable with lighting, music, candles Have a snack or beverage on hand	Enjoy snack or beverage Listen to music Watch a show	Have a snack or beverage Do something fun or enjoyable

What ideas do you have for ways you could boost a task that is hard for you before, during, or after? Feel free to use some of mine or brainstorm your own.

BOOST BEFORE	TWEAK DURING	REWARD AFTER

Another task initiation strategy that can help is to remember that ADHD brains frequently prefer easy-to-start tasks. Is there any way to make one of these hard-to-start tasks just a little bit easier? Can you make the task you are trying to do smaller, shorter, or reduce any obstacles getting in the way?

Emotional Control

Guare, Dawson, and Guare describe emotional control as "the ability to manage emotions in order to help ourselves regulate and guide our behavior, perform tasks, and reach our goals" (2013, 163). This definition highlights how our ability to manage emotions has a large impact on being able to take actions toward our goals. But what does it mean to manage our emotions differently? Working with your emotions skillfully is not just a matter of controlling or managing how you look from the outside, it is a way of relating differently to our emotions.

In her book *Emotional Agility*, David discusses how in our society emotions are labeled "good" or "bad" and this often leads people to try to push away or deny negative feelings they "don't want to have." However, David emphasizes that this denial doesn't work. When emotions are pushed aside or ignored, they become stronger. Eventually, this internal pain comes out in ways we didn't intend. To counter this, we must learn how to manage a variety of emotional responses to help us develop skills to accept our changing reality as it is.

So, how do we relate to our emotions in ways that don't deny them and push them away? First, to begin practicing these skills, it is helpful to practice labeling our emotions and expanding our emotional vocabulary. The more words we have for different emotions, the more clearly we can understand our experiences. It is important to realize that our emotions aren't "the truth," but they are an important source of data about ourselves. In the following case study, Jasmine's emotional agility and control increases after she goes to writing camp and is encouraged to journal authentically about all her feelings.

Jasmine's parents wanted her to be calm and positive because they were dealing with the behavior challenges of her hyperactive-impulsive younger brother. They freaked out if she seemed too anxious or depressed. As a result, she had gotten into a habit of shoving her feelings down or trying to distract herself by watching YouTube. She looked controlled on the outside, but inside was another story. Ruminating thoughts and worries cropped up whenever there was a break in her attention. Sometimes she tried to self-medicate by drinking Diet Coke or eating entire packages of Oreos. One summer, she went to a writing camp and the counselors told her to experiment with writing about her authentic feelings and telling her unique story. The impact of this was incredible for Jasmine—she began understanding herself and her emotions better, and this enabled her to show up with more presence and groundedness in the world. It became easier to process her feelings and experiences, and she was able to find other coping strategies outside of caffeine and sugar.

Do you relate to Jasmine's story, either how she related to her emotions before she began journaling regularly or after?

_____

_____

_____

_____

_____

_____

Is there a safe person in your life, such as a therapist, friend, or parent, with whom you can express your authentic emotions freely?

_____

_____

_____

_____

_____

I'M UNCOMFORTABLE WITH FEELING "BAD" EMOTIONS!

A great way to process your emotions, become more comfortable with them, and have the space to express them is to cultivate a regular journaling practice. Julia Cameron, author of the famous *The Artist's Way* (2016), recommends a daily practice of *morning pages*, which involves three pages of daily longhand freewriting after you wake up.

I have found this practice to be quite helpful in letting me have an outlet for my worries, ruminating thoughts, and other intense emotions. However, my ADHD brain has difficulty writing three pages every morning, so I allow any length of journaling to meet my journaling goal. I try to do it in the morning, but I am also okay with doing it later in the day if that's how the day goes. I also can't always find my notebook, so I also allow myself to type my morning pages if necessary or dictate them into a journaling app that I have on my phone.

Have you ever tried to journal to help process your feelings? How did it go for you? Were you able to stick with the practice, or did you hit obstacles?

_____

_____

_____

_____

If you think journaling is something that might be helpful for you, how could you make it easier? Could you combine it with something you already do (picking up your phone, making a to-do list, a nighttime or morning routine, etc.)?

_____

_____

_____

_____

Goal-Directed Persistence

Many people are surprised that goal-directed persistence, or the ability to keep focused on a goal over time, is a brain-based skill (that is, an executive function). This is the ability to keep focused on a goal consistently over time. This doesn't mean that you never get distracted or take breaks, it just means that you keep coming back to the goal over and over. In the case studies below, Isabella is very goal-driven about her singing and acting career, and she is very determined about her career path. In contrast, Avery has trouble keeping goals in mind and is easily discouraged by perceived failures.

Isabella knows her goal, and she has always known it. She isn't confused about what she wants out of life like some of her friends are. She is going to be an actress, singer, and dancer. Isabella pursues her goal with determination and persistence. When she is given advice or feedback, she implements it. She constantly signs up for classes and works on her skills. When others question the viability of her dream, she lets their comments roll off her back, and does not let herself be swayed.

Avery wants a few things to change, but she doesn't know how to get there. It all sounds hard, and she can never focus. She wants to change her pronouns, and she wants to date Zane. But when she thinks about trying to talk to Zane or explaining her gender identity to everyone, she becomes overwhelmed. Social communication has always been something she has struggled with. She has very few friends outside of the soccer team, and on the soccer team, she knows people think she is bossy and inconsiderate of others at times. Avery worries that people put up with her, so she doesn't feel like she can be herself. She is always afraid of saying something stupid or offensive without meaning to. She would like to change some of these things about her life, but often gets stuck in overwhelm.

Do you relate more to Avery's story about getting overwhelmed with goals or Isabella's story of confidently moving toward an important goal of yours? Do you have a goal you are passionate and pretty certain about, or do you feel somewhat lost?

If you are not sure how to make meaningful goals yet, you are not alone. Many of us struggle to know what calls to us, motivates us, or which goals would feel right. If this is a challenge for you, that's okay. While many of us who struggle with having a goal, do you see any challenges that Isabella could face, even with her goal-directed persistence strength?

_____

_____

_____

_____

_____

_____

If you need a boost in this area, I recommend remembering that goals can be fun. You don't just have to have difficult goals, or school-related goals, or self-improvement goals. You can make a goal to do more fun things or have more downtime or explore an interest! Can you think of a fun goal you might want to work toward in the future? I will not hold you to this...this is just to get you brainstorming!

_____

_____

_____

_____

_____

How Do I Reach a Goal?

Once you've come up with a goal, try to make the process of reaching the goal visual! Can you write down the steps on a whiteboard or track the days you work on the goal, even if you only do it for a super small amount of time, on the calendar? Try to make the steps along the way easy or fun or include frequent celebrations to keep you going!

WHITEBOARD CHECKLIST

Goal: _____

Step 1

Step 2

Step 3

Step 4

You can also use the calendar tracking system to check off each day you work on your goal. Try not to break the streak, but if you miss a day (life happens!), try not to miss two in a row!

Goal: _____

	M	T	W	R	F	SA	SU
Week 1							
Week 2							
Week 3							
Week 4							

Flexibility

Flexibility is the ability to adjust easily to changes in plans and/or approach problems in new and novel ways. While I am flexible with ideas (I can come up with a lot of ideas) and for other people (I am a recovering people pleaser), I was surprised to learn that I am quite inflexible in my behavior and common approaches to my problems. Many of us are surprised to realize that we are inflexible in our behavior or approaches because we may feel that we are flexible in our ideas (we can come up with a lot of ideas) or flexible for others (we are people pleasers). Some of us are inflexible because we believe we must be perfect (a belief known as perfectionism), and can be inflexible in our standards for ourselves and others as a result. Below, Asha struggles with flexibility, while Jasmine carries this as a strength.

Asha feels that every weakness she has is a problem, in the academic setting and in her personal life. Asha is very sensitive to any suggestion that she isn't perfect and becomes very defensive and resistant if ever criticized. If she sees a problem in herself or her school work, Asha works harder. When she noticed she tested poorly, she enrolled in an SAT course. When she realized ADHD was getting in her way, she signed up for all of the treatment options recommended by her doctor. Working hard is her solution to every problem, and Asha throws herself into all of her school work and self-improvement projects without a second thought.

Jasmine had believed that being good at school was the only route to success until she went to a book talk with one of her favorite writers. When she heard her idol discuss how she had barely passed her classes in high school, yet was always diligently working on her craft in her free time, Jasmine began to envision new options for how she could move toward her goal of being a writer. Jasmine felt encouraged that, no matter what happens with school or with college, if she sets aside the time and shows up to do the work, she can find a way to move in the right direction.

In the above stories, we can see that Asha is much less open to approaching problems in new ways, and this in part stems from her perfectionism. In contrast, Jasmine is open to considering new paths toward her goals, even if they aren't what she expected or aren't "perfect." Jasmine is able to accept her challenges in the academic setting and find another route to her dreams.

Do you identify more with Asha or with Jasmine? Do you tend to approach most problems in the same way, or are you able to adjust easily and stay open to trying new approaches?

_____

_____

_____

_____

_____

Do you believe you need to be perfect? If so, what would it mean to you to be perfect? What would being perfect do for you?

_____

_____

_____

_____

_____

_____

HELP! THE STRATEGIES I KEEP USING ARE WEARING ME DOWN!

If you suspect that your go-to strategies in life are wearing you down, you may want to try integrating some flexibility into your approaches. Consider these questions to try approaching your tasks in a new way:

1. Are there any projects or tasks you could take off your list?

2. Could you lower your standards a bit with an area of your life or with a type of task? Could you ask for help?

3. Try listing all of your commitments and prioritizing them by importance to you. You can label the most important, must-do tasks with an A and the "would be nice, but not essential" tasks with a B. Do the A tasks first, and if you need to, you can push off the B tasks for another time or decide to let them go.

4. As you experiment with new approaches to tasks, record how you feel. Is the new approach better than the old one? What might you want to try next?

   If anxiety comes up because you are doing things "differently," try to sit with it. For some of us, it takes a little while to adjust to a new approach. Hang on, you've got this. 😊

Planning and Prioritization

Now we will discuss EF thinking skills, starting with planning and prioritization, which are the dual skills of making a plan for task completion and determining task steps and in what order to do them (Guare, Dawson, and Guare 2013). Planning and prioritizing skills are used frequently in all areas of a teen's life, including home life, social life, academic life, and more. As you'll see, Isabella experiences challenges in this area, while Avery finds these skills to be effortless.

Isabella's mom tells her that she struggles with planning and prioritization because she rarely plans for and prioritizes school assignments. Isabella's dad tells her she needs to "just apply herself" and questions whether she'll be able to rely on singing and acting to pay the bills. Isabella's parents can't understand how she can work so hard in one area of her life but can't seem to translate it to school. Isabella can't explain why, but school is just so hard to manage. She feels completely lacking in motivation and can barely bring herself to make a study plan, not to mention actually study. Her parents have threatened that if she doesn't "work harder" to bring her grades up, they won't allow her to be in the musical this year. Isabella knows she has to find some help.

Avery's mind is very strategic and visual, oriented toward tasks that have what Avery describes as "clear and obvious procedures." These types of processes and tasks are clear and obvious to her, so it is hard to understand how they aren't clear and obvious to others. Avery's mind is well suited to hands-on and STEM classes. Math is easy for her because she can look at the problem, decide on the right formula, and execute. When she is playing soccer or chess, solving math problems, or performing a science experiment, Avery's brain efficiently makes a plan in the moment and prioritizes steps so easily and effortlessly that she almost doesn't notice it happening at all.

Do you relate to Avery, who has a talent for strategic thinking, planning, and prioritization in particular key areas in her life? Or do you relate to Isabella, who struggles with these skills, especially in school settings?

_____

_____

_____

_____

How do you feel about your abilities in the planning and prioritization area? Would you characterize yourself as having strengths or challenges in this area? What makes you think so?

_____

_____

_____

_____

If this is a challenge for you, how might you have compassion for yourself and your unique brain?

_____

_____

_____

_____

_____

_____

_____

PLANNING AND PRIORITIZATION ARE CHALLENGES FOR ME!

For those of us who have challenges with planning and prioritization, decision making may be difficult. For example, I have trouble with decision making because it requires planning in the moment. Often, my brain will try to compensate for my decision-making challenge by ruminating unhelpfully over and over again about something. However, this actually makes it harder to come to a decision. Here's what I do when I am stuck.

1. To get myself out of the rumination cycle, I write down all the things I am trying to decide between on note cards.

2. Then I pick a card. I try to just go with whatever the card says. For me, if I fight the strategy, it's not going to help.

Is there a decision you're trying to make right now, big or small? Describe the decision.

_____

_____

_____

_____

Write down your options on pieces of paper, mix them up, and pick one randomly. That's the decision!

What are your thoughts on this strategy? Do you think it might be helpful for you? (If you like this strategy, but prefer to use your phone or a laptop, you can find apps and websites that provide you with a wheel you can spin to help you make a decision.)

_____

_____

_____

_____

_____

_____

Working Memory

Working memory is the fancy term for our ability to remember things as we go through our daily life. I like to think of this kind of memory as "walking around memory," or the amount of memory we have while we go about our daily tasks. Working memory does not describe our ability to remember things long ago, but instead, "the ability to hold information in memory while performing complex tasks. It incorporates the ability to draw on past learning or experience to apply to the situation at hand or a project in the future" (Guare, Dawson, and Guare 2013, 15). In general, ADHD brains tend to have less memory space available as we go through the day than neurotypical brains. In the examples below, you can see Asha's challenges with working memory. In contrast, this is an EF strength for Isabella.

Asha hyperfocuses on school because she is very concerned about performing well and getting into a good college. Her anxiety orients her on deadlines, assignments, and task lists, to the point that she has difficulty doing things with friends or managing life's details outside of school. Asha's brain is so full with her school tasks that she often has little memory space left for keeping track of her phone, wallet, keys, and other essential items. Asha also frequently picks up her phone or laptop (when she can find them), but once she opens the devices up, she can't remember what she meant to do with them!

Isabella has a great memory for all things related to her interests—song lyrics, melodies, dance steps, audition dates, when to register for drama classes, and so on. Somehow, she can hear the song or see the dance once and it will just be stored in her brain. Isabella also has a great memory related to the people she has interacted with, which supports her stellar social skills. Isabella can remember people's names and details about what they are interested in, and this really helps her get out of a jam when she shows up late or needs to charm a teacher who is disappointed that "she didn't apply herself" to the assignment at hand.

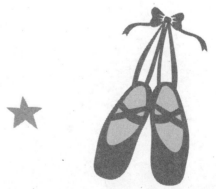

Do you relate to Isabella, who has a strength in working memory, or Asha, who experiences ongoing challenges with it? Or are you somewhere in between? Describe your experiences with working memory.

_____

_____

_____

_____

_____

_____

If you had to rate your working memory on a scale of 1 to 10, what would you rate it? Why? Where do you see your working memory challenges or strengths crop up most?

_____

_____

_____

_____

_____

_____

_____

HELP! I NEED TO BOOST MY WORKING MEMORY!

Whether you want to boost your already awesome memory or cope a little better with major challenges, here are a few strategies that might help you. Mark the ones you might want to try.

★ _____ Say things out loud to yourself to help you remember.

★ _____ Write things down and post reminders where you will see them.

★ _____ Place an item that will remind you of something you want to remember in a place you'll definitely walk past (a visual reminder).

★ _____ Have your phone or Alexa device give you an audible reminder.

★ _____ Make a rhyme. To remember what I could do if I get overwhelmed in a social situation, I made a rhyme to help me remember to take a break and use the bathroom: "When it all gets to be too much, go to where the toilets flush."

★ _____ Make an ad jingle or a song parody to help you remember. You can rewrite the lyrics to remind yourself of something important.

★ _____ Make an acronym. To do this, use the first letter of a few things you want to remember (ideally it spells a word that is also easy to remember).

Scan the list on the previous page. Write "E" next to the easiest strategies to try, "I" next to the most interesting, and "H" next to the most helpful. Now pick one or two to try. I suggest picking an "E" strategy and an "I" strategy because boosting your motivation and lowering your resistance really helps when trying something new!

_____

_____

_____

Which two strategies did you pick? What drew you to those two? When and where might you try them?

_____

_____

_____

_____

_____

_____

Time Management

Time management involves understanding how much time you have, determining where to spend that time, and operating within time limits to meet deadlines. To master these skills, you first have to foster a sense of time and how long things take. This can be tough for some of us and a strength for others, as all EFs are. If time management is a struggle for you, you might find that you lose track of time, have difficulty arriving when expected for appointments, or turn homework in late. In the examples below, we see that Asha has strong time management skills while Isabella's brain struggles with this EF skill.

Asha builds her life around deadlines. She writes them down immediately and begins working on schoolwork way in advance. She has a pretty good sense of how long things will take, but her anxiety frequently encourages her to work on school tasks for longer than might be needed. She always shows up on time for class because she doesn't want to cause any trouble or have anyone think she is not a super serious student. Asha has the deadlines for college applications pretty much seared in her brain, even though it causes her great anxiety when she thinks about it.

Isabella loses track of time when she is getting ready for school. She doesn't mean to, but as she applies her makeup and picks out the right clothes, time seems to speed up in a super frustrating way. It is hard for Isabella to estimate how long these tasks will take, and she always tries to fit "one more thing" in before leaving. "One more thing" is tempting because showing up early and waiting around sounds boring to Isabella. Luckily, Isabella can typically use her social skills to advocate for herself to minimize relationship challenges with her teachers.

Do you relate more to Asha's experience or Isabella's experience?

_____

_____

_____

_____

_____

How would you describe your experience of time management?

TIME MANAGEMENT SUBSKILLS	STRENGTH	CHALLENGE	NOT SURE/ SO-SO
Arriving on time			
Estimating how long tasks will take			
Meeting deadlines			
Caring about time, believing time is important			
Time awareness, sense that time is passing			

HELP! I NEED TO IMPROVE MY TIME MANAGEMENT SKILLS!

If you struggle with time management, take heart! Time management is definitely an EF skill that can be learned and improved upon. 😊 Here is a simple time management strategy I often use to help me plan my week ahead.

1. First, gather information about any deadlines or appointments coming up during the next week. To do this, you'll want to seek out this information wherever it lives. You might have to grab your calendar, scan your syllabus/online class portal, or ask your parent if they keep track of your calendar events.

2. Do you have any assignments, meetings, or events where you have to be somewhere at a specific time? Write them down in a place that helps you remember (notebook, paper calendar, electronic calendar, whiteboard).

3. Now, work backward from those anchor points. Do you need to prepare or study for any of the deadlines, appointments, or events above? When will you do that? Go back to the sketched-out week and fill in what's on your to-do list for those days. Note when you'll start to prepare for the deadlines, appointments, or events.

4. For a bonus challenge, try estimating how long tasks will take as you go. Then compare how long it actually took with your estimation. By employing this as a common practice, you will strengthen your time estimation skills and build a strong foundation for future time management.

A fun way to work on your time management skills is to give yourself a time challenge.

1. Set a timer for how long you want to spend on a task and then challenge yourself to meet the time limit and move on.

2. If you have trouble remembering what you're doing, you might write yourself a note where you can see it while completing the task.

Goal: Clean as much of my room as I can in 15 minutes!

Organization

Organization is the ability to keep track of and maintain systems for our stuff, paperwork, electronic documents, and important tasks. Social expectations often dictate that girls should be organized, so girls and women who struggle to clean up, organize their meals, or complete self-care routines may receive negative feedback from others or be misunderstood by them. They may also internalize these negative messages as part of the inner critic in their minds, becoming very self-critical when they make an organizational mistake or can't "get it together."

You may find that the way you organize things makes sense to you but doesn't look how others expect. That still counts as you having a brain that is geared toward being organized and has organizational strengths! What works for you won't always work for others, and that is okay. The goal of organization is that it is helpful for you, not that it looks nice to others. If you know where your papers and things are and get your important tasks done (whether it is executed as a predictable routine or not), you still have some key organizational strengths that are helping you succeed! In the first example below, we see that Avery has a way of organizing her stuff that she understands but her mother doesn't. In contrast, Jasmine is organized with her tasks but her room is very messy.

Avery has a specific way of organizing her stuff that makes sense to her. She makes piles of papers and books that are sorted into categories that are meaningful to her (for example, current papers, books she wants to read later, and so on). Avery also lays out her soccer stuff in front of the door so seeing it will help her remember to take it with her when she leaves for school. Avery knows where everything is and functions quite successfully in finding her necessary things when she needs them, but her room still looks like a mess. Her mom is constantly nagging her to "clean up" and "put things away!" Avery knows her mother means well, but she doesn't understand why her mother can't see that this system is well thought out, intentional, and works for her ADHD brain.

Jasmine is messy. Her room looks like a bomb has gone off. Clothes, books, papers, makeup, and food wrappers are littered around the room, some consolidated into piles, and others not. She isn't sure why this happens. Somehow, she just picks something up, starts doing something, and then starts doing something else. At the end of the day, everything is a mess. However, Jasmine is queen of the to-do list. She has an academic planner and she writes down her school deadlines and top three tasks for school each day. However, Jasmine's knack of list-making doesn't always translate into her doing the tasks. People are surprised that Jasmine's room is a mess since she seems generally on top of her important tasks.

Can you relate to how Avery organizes her stuff? Do you have a system that works well for you but looks odd to other people?

Does Jasmine sound more like you? Are you organized with lists, but not with your things?

_____

_____

_____

Which of the following activities or items are easy for you to organize? Which are more difficult? Circle somewhere between 1 and 5 if the task is easy and between 6 and 10 if the task is more difficult (1 being most easy and 10 being most difficult).

Tasks	1	2	3	4	5	6	7	8	9	10
Papers	1	2	3	4	5	6	7	8	9	10
Routines	1	2	3	4	5	6	7	8	9	10
Things	1	2	3	4	5	6	7	8	9	10

 # I CAN'T CLEAN MY ROOM!

While it may sound simple, the task of "cleaning your room" is actually quite complex and can be open-ended if you don't have an idea of the steps or a clear plan. For some of us, we struggle to know where to start. If this is you, I recommend trying to break down the task into the categories of stuff that you'll be cleaning up.

1. First, take stock of the types of stuff you'll be cleaning up and make a list (it may include trash, recycling, dirty clothes, clean clothes, plates, and so on).

2. Second, gather your cleaning supplies (trash bag, recycling bin if you'll need it).

3. Third, begin tackling the task by categories. If you find items that don't belong (for example, plates need to be taken back to the kitchen), leave them in a pile by the door and return them at the end of the task. If you leave your room, you're more likely to get distracted by other rooms, so it is wise to remain in your room until the cleaning session is over.

4. Be flexible! If you start losing focus, you don't necessarily have to make yourself finish the whole room. You can complete as many categories (or subtasks of the larger task) at a time you choose. Every little bit of cleaning helps, and it doesn't have to come out perfect! Doing something is definitely better than doing nothing when it comes to ADHD and cleaning! 😊

Which of these steps have you already been doing? Which might you want to try in the future?

_____

_____

_____

_____

_____

_____

What, if any, other strategies or steps would you want to investigate to make your room-cleaning routine more motivating, fun, or effective?

_____

_____

_____

_____

_____

_____

_____

_____

_____

Metacognition

Metacognition is the ability to reflect on our experiences, learn from that information, and apply it in the future. Metacognition is a complex executive function. This skill includes seeing the big picture of a situation and the ability to ask yourself how you are doing. Metacognition saves you quite a bit of time in the long run if you develop a habit of reflecting on your goals and progress. In the examples below, Avery shows what it looks like to struggle with metacognition while Jasmine's metacognition is improving over time as she practices journaling.

Avery struggles with metacognition when she is involved in a task that she can easily focus on, like soccer, chess, or math. When she is "inside the task," as she describes it, she loses track of how she comes across to others. Avery gets so focused on the task at hand, and using the right strategy, that she doesn't realize that others find her bossy and demanding. Others also find it hard to be friendly with her because Avery is always so serious, focusing 100 percent of her energy and awareness on winning the game or getting the task done. Because Avery's brain only sees the "now" and the "not now," once Avery is done with a task, she is completely mentally done with it.

Jasmine's metacognition improves every time she journals. By journaling, she becomes more able to view her problems from a wider lens. Whereas she used to freak out when she faced school challenges, she now is able to step back, process her feelings, and brainstorm some options. She could get a tutor to help her with math and science, and she could find someone to help her with how to break down her writing assignments. Now that she has gotten her diagnosis and is in the process of getting some accommodations at school, she feels more optimistic. Maybe she will ask the school counselor about tutoring and help for writing assignments. The counselor is nice and nonjudgmental and could likely help her think of some good next steps.

Do you relate more to Avery or to Jasmine? Are you able to zoom out and see the big picture of the situations that you're a part of, either in real time or after the fact?

_____

_____

_____

_____

_____

How often do you stop and self-evaluate the way Jasmine does? Is it an easy or hard thing to do? What, if anything, gets in the way of you doing this?

_____

_____

_____

_____

_____

_____

_____

METACOGNITION IS A STRUGGLE FOR ME!

What I love about the metacognition superpower is that it's pretty accessible to work on, and there are a lot of options regarding how to work on it. Every time you work on this workbook, go to therapy, process your experiences with a friend, or write in your journal, you are strengthening this key skill. Whether this reflective ability feels like something you come by easily or not, it is well worth your time to brainstorm a way that you could develop it. It supports so many EF skills and your general self-awareness, which is essential to your ability to thrive with ADHD (this is what we'll be working on in the next chapter).

Which of the following strategies might you try? Circle the most appealing strategies.

★ Reflect on your experiences in a workbook.

★ Go to therapy and process your feelings and thoughts with a mental health professional.

★ Try new strategies and reflect on what went well and what didn't go well (and why) with a friend or an EF skills/ADHD coach.

★ Regularly journal by typing on a computer or writing in a notebook.

★ Dictate your ideas in a journaling app or in voice memos on your phone.

★ Reread or relisten to your journal entries, looking for themes, new takeaways, and progress.

★ Check in with yourself weekly to reflect on what went well the previous week and what you'd like to tweak. Make a plan to continue with the successes and improve what needs tweaking.

CHAPTER SUMMARY

CONTENT SUMMARY

✔ Try to remember that we all have EF strengths and challenges. Our challenges don't cancel out our strengths. We can be working to improve some of our challenges *and* appreciate our impressive strengths *at the same time.*

✔ Next, review the EF definitions in the table below and consolidate what you learned about your strengths and challenges in the different EF areas with the scorecard. Your particular strengths and challenges will be helpful information for you to remember moving forward. Rate whether each executive function is a strength ("S"), a challenge ("C"), or it depends ("D"). You'll also find a copy of this chart at the website for this book: http://www.newharbinger.com/52809. You can come back to this chart over time as you gain self-awareness and are better able to notice how your behavior relates to EF skills.

YOUR EXECUTIVE FUNCTION SCORECARD		
EXECUTIVE FUNCTION	**DEFINITION**	**S, C, OR D**
Sustained Attention	Being able to focus despite feeling bored or tired	
Response Inhibition	The ability to pause before acting to make sure your actions are intentional	
Task Initiation	The ability to get started on a variety of tasks	
Emotional Control	Managing emotions to be able to follow through, behave in expected ways, and move toward your goals	
Goal-Directed Persistence	The ability to move toward a multistep goal	
Flexibility	The ability to adjust to changes in plans and try out new approaches and behaviors	
Planning/ Prioritization	The ability to make a plan and prioritize actions that will move the plan forward	
Working Memory	Holding information in your mind while you go about your daily life; being able to apply previous information and experiences to the situation at hand	
Time Management	The ability to know how much time you have, determine where to spend that time, operate within time limits, and meet deadlines	
Organization	The ability to keep track of and maintain systems for stuff, paperwork, electronic documents, and important tasks	
Metacognition	The ability to reflect on your experiences and carry that information forward to apply it in the future	

STRATEGY SUMMARY

⭐ If you struggle with planning too much or not enough, you might try intentionally separating the planning task from the doing task and then give yourself a clear planning goal or time limit.

⭐ Taking regularly scheduled short breaks can help manage your hyperfocus.

⭐ Pairing a task with something pleasant can help with getting started on it (not to mention your desire to continue on).

⭐ Learning to experience, name, and develop a robust vocabulary around your emotions can help with emotional control.

⭐ Making a visual tracking system (this can be very simple!) can help with follow-through on important, multistep goals.

⭐ Try lowering your standards, or raising them. Try doing the opposite of what you would normally do and see what happens.

⭐ If you have trouble with decision making, write out the options and pick a random card.

⭐ If you have working memory issues, try visual, written, or auditory reminders. Get creative with rhymes, acronyms, or song parodies to help you remember things.

⭐ For time management issues, look ahead to your deadlines and prepare a schedule. Practice estimating how long something will take and then comparing it to how long it actually took.

⭐ Cleaning tasks can be made easier by tackling one category of stuff at a time. Remember: You don't have to do all the categories at once. Every little bit counts. 😄

⭐ Find an easy and accessible way of regularly reflecting on your experiences and what you've learned.

CHAPTER 4

SELF-KNOWLEDGE AND ACCEPTANCE

Self-knowledge and acceptance are very important to foster but they can be hard to check off a list or always be able to tell if we're making progress on them. This is a journey within the larger journey, as our knowledge and acceptance of ourselves will evolve and deepen over time. In this chapter, I have included some activities to help you get started. If this is the first time you've done this, it may feel uncomfortable, overwhelming, and uncertain to think about what's important to you and who you are. If that's the case, I encourage you to take breaks and slow down, even almost to a crawl if you need to. I hope you will not give up entirely, though.

I believe that I am as I am meant to be, and you are as you are meant to be. I believe that you have something wonderfully unique to offer us, if you can continue the work of knowing and accepting yourself. I believe that against all odds, we are both here and that fact has *meaning*. I can't claim to know what the meaning is for you. I'm not even 100 percent sure I know what my meaning is, but I am finding pieces to my puzzle and putting them together. I have a feeling that slowly, yet surely, the meaning of my life is emerging.

Authors Sari Solden and Michelle Frank (2019) taught me that the purpose of life is not to *fix* oneself but to *be* oneself. Martha Beck, a well-known author and life coach, says that, just like a plane must be in integrity with all its parts or it might crash, we are the same. She says, "When you experience unity of intention, fascination, and purpose, you live like a bloodhound on a scent, joyfully doing what feels truest in each moment" (Beck 2021, xii). So how do we figure out what we are meant to be doing and who we really are? Well, if it were easy, everyone would do it. You and I would have done it already! And if it is so important, then why is it so hard and what is getting in the way, gosh darnit?!

ACTIVITY 27

Accept Where Your Life Is Now

If you feel life is hard for you, it is not that you are doing it wrong. It is that life is hard for everyone. "Really?" you ask. "But my friend makes it look so easy and celebrities have fabulous lives!" Believe me, despite what you see on the face of things, life is hard for everyone. If not today, then someday. Or they are just keeping it all inside.

Sometimes we get the sense that we could just act like someone else if we want to. Just like exchanging a top at the store, we could just pretend to have other character traits. We hope that if we could just figure out which traits people like and then act as if we have them, we'd have made it. This is called masking. You can certainly try to do this. I did. Lots of us do. At first, it seems like a good idea. We will adopt the traits that are praised, and then people will like us. Then we will be perfect and be happy. In the short term this performance may work, but in the long term there are unforeseen consequences. You start to lose connection with yourself. You put on a performance, but you aren't even that good at it because it isn't real. Even if you are good at it for a while, eventually the cracks start to show. Also since you aren't being real, other people who share your interests can't find you. The real you can't find you either. You may start to feel disillusioned, hopeless, depressed. The costs of the performance mount. Eventually, the cracks begin to show.

The good news is that when the cracks show, we are often motivated to change. Sometimes it takes all of that trial and error to figure out what works for us and what doesn't. It's totally understandable and valid if you decide to put on a mask to get by, and it's totally valid if you decide to save yourself time and work on getting to know yourself now. Or somewhere in between is fine too, because it isn't always easy to tell when we're performing and when we're not, when we're running toward something and when we're just running away from a negative outcome we don't like (not being popular, feeling unworthy, and so on). In the following story about Jasmine, you'll see how connecting with someone who had a similar experience helped her accept challenging aspects of her life.

Jasmine likes to pretend that her life is different. She doesn't mean to do this—it's subconscious—but this is how she approaches her life to cope with a reality she struggles to accept. She doesn't want to have a chaotic home environment with a hyperactive-impulsive brother who sucks up all the energy and resources in her home. She doesn't want to have stressed-out parents who work all the time or pay all of their attention to her little brother, but she does. She doesn't want to feel that when she starts to struggle her parents have no capacity to help her, and she can see how she just adds to their already full list of stressors and to-dos. Jasmine's parents want her to be the "easy" one since her brother is not. Jasmine got in the habit of pretending to be fine long ago when it became clear that there was no space for her needs.

When Jasmine has to get a peer math tutor at school, she never expected that Avery would have ADHD too and would have similar home life dynamics in reverse. Avery is the "problem child" in her home. Somehow, learning about Avery's home experiences created space for Jasmine to feel more acceptance for her own family. Jasmine is also realizing that her life might provide great reading material—her writing teacher was raving about her latest writing piece in which she described an incident between her brother and her parents!

Does Jasmine's role as the "good girl" in the family resonate with you? Or do you connect more to Avery's story of being the "difficult sibling" in her home? How do you think ADHD might affect the role you play in your family?

_____

_____

_____

_____

How do your ADHD symptoms show up at home? How do they show up at school? Do you face challenges in one setting more than the other, or face challenges in both equally? What makes you think this?

_____

_____

_____

_____

_____

_____

I WANT A DIFFERENT LIFE!

It can be easy to wish that we had different talents, challenges, or life circumstances. We can dream of the ease of being good at everything. I have often fallen into this mental and emotional trap, wishing I was more like the popular pretty girls or the girls who seem to clearly have it "all together."

What if we could somehow pivot from seeing our lives, circumstances, and challenges as something we might like to exchange to seeing all these things as so very interesting? We love interesting things, after all.

If you were to tell me an interesting story about your life, what would you tell? Would you tell me about your triumphs, your struggles? Would you present yourself as the same as everyone else or different and unique?

_____

_____

_____

_____

_____

Is there a problem you have, something that really annoys you? What about this problem is compelling or interesting to you? What about it might make an interesting story that others could connect to?

_____

_____

_____

_____

_____

Who Is on Your Bus?

The metaphor of driving a bus is used in acceptance and commitment therapy to help us visualize the complexity of what is going on in our brains when we are driving along, trying to get where we're going. Many of us have inner critics riding on the bus, motivated by fear and a desire to keep us safe. These inner critics may represent different people we've come across or messages we've internalized. In internal family systems therapy, another prominent type of therapy, we learn that inside ourselves, we can have multiple and conflicting parts. These different parts or "personas" are the passengers on our bus.

Some of us are very uncomfortable with all this noise and try to push these negative voices or personas we don't like away. What can help is realizing that even though these negative thoughts feel real, they are not who we really are. We can learn how to gain some space from these thoughts and continue on, heading toward where we want to go. If we are able to relax, take a step back and use our metacognitive skill to analyze our inner critic's messages, we can start to learn more about ourselves and the stories we've internalized. In the example below, Isabella does this with her therapist.

Isabella suspects that her parents put her in therapy because they don't know what to do with her. She likes it sometimes when she can just vent, but it is hard not to be annoyed at all the time it takes when the therapist decides to "teach" her something. Inner eye roll. Despite her internal complaints, Isabella projects calm and charm in the therapy session. At this particular session, the therapist starts talking about the stupid bus metaphor again. Isabella completes another inner eye roll paired with a polished smile on the outside. "Who is on your bus?" the therapist asks. "Who is on my bus?" Isabella clarifies. "What?" The therapist is patient. "The passengers on the bus often represented inner messages you've internalized from your parents, social media, your school, and so on. There is often more than one passenger because we can have multiple voices or messages in our heads." "Is it like characters in a play, their internal monologues?" Isabella asks. "Pretty much like that." her therapist responds. "Well," says Isabella, "I'm not sure about all the passengers, but I'm pretty sure my dad's voice is there somewhere. Maybe he would be a drill sergeant. With some sort of whistle. He just repeats the same commands over and over, never hearing anybody else." "That's a great start, Isabella," says the therapist.

What voices echo in your head? Do you think messages from family, teachers, friends, or social media creep in?

_____

_____

_____

_____

_____

HELP! MY INNER CRITICS ARE SO LOUD!

Some of us have very vocal inner critics, and this can be quite frustrating. You might find that giving your passengers names, personas, or identities helps you distance yourself from these critical or inflexible messages and helps you learn how to work with them moving forward. If labeling your inner critic or giving them a persona doesn't seem to help, you might try a different approach of accepting your inner critic. For most of us, our inner critic is an anxious and childlike part of us who is trying to keep us safe. We can show our critic some compassion, thank them for trying to help us, but then let them know that they can step off the bus because we've got it from here. In her book *Big Magic* (2015), Elizabeth Gilbert acknowledges that her inner critic will always be a passenger in her life as she works on creative projects. When she begins a book, Gilbert announces to the inner critic that she is welcome to ride along but that she will "never drive."

How might you accept your inner critic or critics but make it clear to them that you, not them, will be driving? Put another way, how can you accept their inevitable presence, but show them that you are in charge of your bus?

_____

_____

_____

_____

_____

How Satisfied Are You?

In this section, you'll assess how you feel about your life right now. You'll reflect on how satisfied you in are different areas of your life, such as home, school, social life, extracurricular activities, and self-confidence. Your personal satisfaction matters, and it is an important piece of maintaining your stamina and helping you move toward your goals. Though it may seem counterintuitive, placing your own needs front and center will make it easier to perform better and more easily relate to others.

During the teen years, it can be all too easy to get lost in the numerous expectations of our teachers, parents, and friends. We are often told to work harder to keep up rather than focusing on our own needs. While it may seem like it wastes time to tend to ourselves, ultimately we will burn out if we don't take our own needs into account.

This short survey asks you to rate your satisfaction in different areas of your life. This is a commonly used tool that coaches and therapists use when working with people who want to improve their lives. When I ask you to reflect on your *satisfaction*, I am asking you to check your gut feelings about whether your personal needs are being met. In case the term "satisfaction" doesn't resonate with you or you feel like you don't know what that means, you could substitute the word "contentment," "enjoyment," or "engagement," or come up with your own alternative word. To be clear: I am not asking about your performance in these areas or about your mother or father or friend's opinion about how you are doing. I am asking you to reflect on the following: When you think of the different areas of your life, how content, joyful, and satisfied do you feel in this area?

When you take this survey, try to tap into your intuition, and don't overthink it. If you need to set a timer to keep yourself moving and not get stuck ruminating, go for it. The advantage of rating yourself in this exercise is that you can come back to this survey later to see how well your hard work is paying off. This can help you see whether your numbers have changed and can provide a springboard for reflecting on your progress. You'll find a copy of this survey at the website for this book: http://www .newharbinger.com/52809.

LIFE SATISFACTION SURVEY	
AREA OF LIFE	**CIRCLE YOUR SATISFACTION NUMBER ON A SCALE OF 1 TO 10 (1 BEING LOWEST, 10 BEING HIGHEST)**
Home life and family relationships	1 2 3 4 5 6 7 8 9 10
School life	1 2 3 4 5 6 7 8 9 10
Afterschool activities and hobbies	1 2 3 4 5 6 7 8 9 10
Social and romantic life	1 2 3 4 5 6 7 8 9 10
Self-confidence	1 2 3 4 5 6 7 8 9 10

Which area are you most satisfied with? Which area are you least satisfied with?

_____

_____

_____

_____

Are you surprised about your results? Why or why not?

_____

_____

_____

_____

Perhaps you feel that focusing on your satisfaction is a waste of time. Asha did too.

Asha was struggling with feeling down most of the time, and it was getting in the way of her college application plans, so she did a quick Google search for an ADHD coach and started to reach out. She wasn't sure whether she should talk to a coach or a therapist about this, but she figured that the coach could probably help her sort that out and she just needed to do *something*. This lack of motivation during the fall of her senior year simply would not do for Asha.

Her ADHD coach asked her to rate her satisfaction in a short survey. Asha wasn't sure what it meant to be satisfied. She didn't see how this would help her get into a good college. She knew what didn't make her feel satisfied—studying all the time, feeling stressed out by all she had to do. Even when she did well on an assignment, she felt depleted, knowing that there were a zillion other items on her high school and college prep to-do list. Her coach asked, "What would you rate school? How satisfied are you?" Asha sighed, wondering why she had thought it was a good idea to try coaching. Finally, she said, "I would give it a 3 because I do like choir and drama, and I have some friends at school too." "Okay," said the coach. "What would bring up your satisfaction to a 4 or even higher?" Asha said, "I want to study less, have more fun, obsess less about assignments." "Those are great goals!" enthused the coach. "Let's figure out how to get you there!"

Can you relate to how Asha feels about school? Do you like talking about/taking surveys on satisfaction or do you find it boring or annoying?

_____

_____

_____

_____

_____

NOTHING FEELS SATISFYING TO ME!

If you are taking this survey, and struggling to find anything satisfying, or feel like it's just too hard to do anything to increase your satisfaction, I recommend reaching out for help. It is common for girls with ADHD to experience co-occurring mood issues, so if you're recognizing you've been feeling down for awhile and it's getting in the way of your goals, consider asking for help from a therapist, coach, or school counselor who can work with you or help you figure out a good next step.

If reaching out to ask for help feels overwhelming, is there someone in your life who could help you take a first step in contacting someone?

ACTIVITY 30

Managing Social Expectations

What often gets in the way of knowing ourselves is all of the expectations for teens today. When you are under ten, you are mostly expected to play and do well enough at social interaction. For some of us this is already difficult, and for others of us it is doable. For me, I had one friend and did fine in school. Not much else was expected, and I had a lot of time to do what I wanted, play, and have fun. During middle school, the expectations went up quite a bit and that was when I started to struggle significantly.

If you are struggling with all the expectations, you should know that you are not the problem and you are not alone. Even if you were perfect (and nobody is), you wouldn't be able to meet all the expectations because there are just too many. It is helpful to be aware of all the unattainable expectations placed on girls so that you don't fall into the common traps of trying to meet them all through perfectionism, people-pleasing, and overworking. Trying to do everything that is expected of girls these days is more likely to result in depression, anxiety, and poor mental health, rather than an ability to meet all expectations. Instead, you can decide what is most important to you and let some other things go. Here is a list of the expectations that are placed on teen girls today.

- Being healthy and fit
- Academics and being smart
- Making and maintaining friendships
- Romance and dating
- College and career planning
- Being organized
- Keeping your room clean

- Self-care
- Having a job
- Managing emotions
- Obeying parents and maintaining family relationships
- Participating in extracurricular activities

Can you think of any others? What are they?

_____

_____

_____

Scanning the list of social expectations above, which do you find most easy to meet, if any? Which are most difficult to meet?

_____

_____

_____

_____

_____

Is meeting social expectations important to you? What are the pros and cons of trying to meet social expectations?

_____

_____

_____

_____

Since this list is impossibly long, which of these expectations do you think you might want to take off your plate? Which are the least important to you?

_____

_____

_____

_____

In the case study below, Isabella has to choose between meeting social expectations and pursuing her personal interests.

Isabella is burned out on school and all the pressure during the fall of her junior year. She doesn't really want to go to college right away, but apparently *everyone* else is, so her parents are making her take the tests, work on her grades, and so on. She just wants to get ready for the high school musical and figure out all that school and college stuff later. Everyone is so jacked up about adulthood...why are they so worried?! She'll figure it out. Isabella can tell her parents just want her to be one of those super smart National Merit kids so they can brag to other parents: "Look at me, my child is SO successful, just like yours." She doesn't want to disappoint her parents, she knows they have done a lot for her, but she wants to enjoy her high school experience while it is here.

What would you advise Isabella to prioritize here? Her personal interests or the expectations of others? Or would you advise her to try and find a way of balancing both by scaling back her expectations for herself in one or both of these areas?

_____

_____

_____

_____

HELP! I CAN'T STOP TRYING TO BE PERFECT AND DO IT ALL!

Even when we know logically we can't be perfect, it can still be difficult not to wish we were or work hard to be. We may even idealize perfection (I know I have), imagining that if we were perfect, life would be easier. Our brains may even assume that if we were perfect, we wouldn't have to struggle and people would like us more. I have come to realize that even if perfection was attainable, there is no guarantee that life would be easier. I might actually be bored with perfection! It's possible that people would like me more if I were perfect, but it's also possible that others would like me less, finding me less relatable and a more robust target for their envy.

If you are struggling with this, you are not alone. It takes a lot of practice to slow down, work on self-acceptance, and to try not to fall into the trap of perfectionism. If you want to remind yourself to strive for good enough and then move on, you can use the acronym GEMO created by Elaine Taylor-Klaus and Diane Dempster (2016) as a mantra: *Good enough, move on!*

If you could be "perfect" and "do it all," what do you think it would do for you? How do you imagine you would feel? Do you think it would really be as wonderful as many people think?

_____

_____

_____

_____

_____

What are the pros and cons of striving for perfection? What are the pros and cons of striving for good enough and then moving on when you've reached it?

_____

_____

_____

_____

_____

_____

_____

_____

Accepting Change

Some of us resist changes in our lives because they are not what we expected or wanted. Sometimes we think other people have it easier, or we expect life to look like the images we see in movies or on social media. We rail against our reality, our thoughts going on mental loops about how things should be different, we should be different, we did not sign up for this. In our dissatisfaction, we might try to escape reality or distract ourselves. We might try to identify what is wrong about our life and set about on an impossible quest to fix it. Byron Katie (2021), a well-known author, asserts that reality is always "right." She points out that our realities exist outside of our control. She recommends that in order to accept our realities, we should become adept at questioning our beliefs about how things should be different than they really are. This is a process that can help us identify when social messages are shaping our expectations in unhelpful ways.

A key step in accepting our changing realities is first identifying our thoughts and then asking ourselves whether they are true. See how Isabella does this work with her therapist below.

Isabella is devastated. She didn't get the lead role in the musical. After she got the news, she began spiraling, angry thoughts echoing in her head: "This should be easier, I must have no talent. I can't take all of this rejection. This isn't fair." Isabella's stress response is on high alert so she is grateful she will see her therapist today. Crying and balling up her fists, Isabella repeats the thoughts that keep playing over and over again: "This isn't fair. This should be easier. I must be terrible." The therapist says, "It's completely normal to be sad and disappointed. It's okay to have these feelings." "I don't want these feelings, they feel awful," Isabella says. "I have an idea that might help," says the therapist. "Are you calm enough to be able to try a new strategy?" "I will try anything!" Isabella says, but then realizes that her emotions might be running too high for her to be able to focus. "But I should probably go to the bathroom and get a drink of water before I do." "Great idea," says the therapist. When Isabella returns, she still seems shaken but is visibly more collected. "Okay, I'm ready to try the strategy." The therapist says, "I heard you say that this isn't fair, this should be easier, and you must be terrible. Do you think those statements are really true?" Isabella is about to say yes, but then she realizes they aren't always true. "I was going to say yes, but I know on some level that the person who got the role is really good, works really hard, and that I am good too. She is a senior, so she doesn't have another shot at it, whereas I do. I can try again next year." Isabella's therapist compliments Isabella for being able to revise her narrative about the situation to make it more true.

Have you ever reacted to a rejection like Isabella did at first? What thoughts went on a loop in that moment? Were those thoughts true? If those thoughts weren't true, can you think of some modifications to the thoughts that would make them more accurate?

_____

_____

_____

_____

_____

HOW DO I CALM DOWN AND COMFORT MYSELF?

When reality is not as we planned or expected, or we feel rejected or dissapointed, it may be helpful to stop and comfort ourselves before trying to take action. In those moments, it can be helpful to have a list of things that are comforting to us when we are upset. Here are some ideas:

- ★ Taking a bath

- ★ Reading or listening to a book or podcast

- ★ Watching a video clip

- ★ Drinking a warm beverage

- ★ Sitting underneath a weighted blanket

- ★ Listening to music

- ★ Talking to a trusted friend, family member, or therapist

- ★ Dancing to a favorite song with an inspiring message. When I feel criticized, I like dancing to Taylor Swift's "Shake It Off"

Have you tried any of the comfort activities listed above when you want to take a step back or calm down? How, if at all, have the activities you've tried helped you in the past? Would you add any activities to your list?

_____

_____

_____

_____

What Is Important to You?

A big part of knowing yourself well is knowing what is important to you. If you're not sure what is important to you *yet*, don't worry or feel bad. It is possible that no one has ever asked you to reflect on this. It's also possible that your fast, busy brain finds this to be a tough question to answer, and if that's the case, you are definitely not alone in that. Every effort you make in the direction of knowing yourself and who you are helps you in the long run, even if it isn't always easy. We don't choose our values; they are just part of who we are. At times, it is hard to tell what is important to us unless we slow down and listen inside of ourselves. I know, this can be hard for our ADHD brains! However, with practice, you will get better and better and see the work pay off.

So how do we get better at listening to ourselves? How do we read the hard-to-decipher signs? Well, for starters, certain emotions can be clues that can help us determine our values. For example, joy, enthusiasm, contentment, anxiety, apprehension, or frustration may point us toward something about a situation that moves us in line with or away from our values. Extreme emotions may be more about showing us our stress response, but the more subtle emotions we experience can often tip us off to our values if we are able to practice listening to them. It can be difficult at times to stop and look at our emotional responses, but as we learn to decode these internal sensations, we will start to build a solid foundation of self-knowledge over time.

Another way to think about our values is to search for situations that "trigger" us because they make us feel something in a negative way or situations that represent "glimmers," or times we feel really good.

Try to remember a time you felt contented, joyful, or enthusiastic, an experience that you might label a "glimmer." The experience can be big or small. What were you doing at the time? Were you by yourself or were other people there? Draw or describe the situation with sensory details so you can really remember what contributed to your positive feelings.

Now, think of a time you felt anxious, apprehensive, or frustrated. Again, the experience can be big or small. What were you doing at the time? Were you by yourself or with others? What "triggered" you about the situation? Draw or describe the situation with sensory details so you can really remember what contributed to your difficult feelings. (If you need to a take a break because this is a challenging thing to write about, that's okay. You can always come back to it later.) ☺

Reread or look over your glimmer and your trigger above. Pretend that someone else is showing you these drawings or telling you these stories. Pretend that you are standing outside yourself so you can get some distance and be able to analyze the information. Based on what you read or saw, what do you think is important, meaningful, supportive, enjoyable, or comforting to this person? What is stressful or challenging for this person? What is this person good at? What does this person struggle with? Brainstorm some ideas in the following chart, or circle some terms below if you get stuck. All the ideas you come up with and the circled words on the following page will help point you toward your personal values.

CIRCLE IDEAS HERE	BRAINSTORM YOUR IDEAS HERE
Learning	
Looking good	
Authenticity	
Hard work	
Loyalty	
Letting loose	
Hobbies	
Dreams	
Mental health	
Physical health	
Fun	
Personal interests	
Downtime	
Peace	
Friendship	
Family	
Good grades	

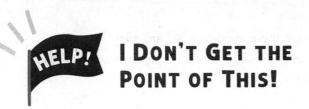

HELP! I Don't Get the Point of This!

If you feel like the concept of values is a bit abstract, you are not alone. Sometimes it can be hard to figure out how a short list of words can help us in our everyday lives. The idea is that creating a values list will make it easier to remember what matters to you in a highly distracting world. If you post your values somewhere easy to find them, or take a picture on your phone, or put a notecard in your wallet, you will have something to refer to when you are having difficulty knowing what to do next. Many people find that referencing their values can help them prioritize and make decisions. You can even start a daily check-in where you look at your list and reflect on whether you've been living by your values recently. Completing the questions below will help you get started on what this kind of regular reflection might look like.

Can you reflect on a time when you've felt like you've been doing things that are important to you or living your values? What did that feel like and how did you know?

_____

_____

_____

_____

Can you think of a time when you knew you weren't living your values? What did that feel like and how did you know?

_____

_____

_____

_____

Consider keeping a list of your values posted so you can see them everyday. Where might you put them so you can be reminded? Would you carry the list in your wallet, or take a picture and store it in your phone? When might you plan to check in with your list?

_____

_____

_____

_____

What Inspires You? What Are Your Dreams?

Continuing to be who we are is not easy as we navigate life changes, changing expectations, well-meaning but unhelpful advice, and environments that may or may not be supportive for our ADHD brains. To stay on the right path as much as possible, try to keep an eye out for anything that sparks, inspires, or interests you, no matter how small or seemingly silly (Solden and Frank 2019). These sparks are clues to what is meaningful to us, whether it is something fun to do along the way, something we might want to do for work, or something we have to offer the world. If you can, you might try having a folder, a box, or an app on your phone where you can store anything that inspires you. Feel free to save clues in whatever form is easiest or works best—take pictures, screenshots, dictate your thoughts or ideas, keep a small notebook in your pocket. You don't have to share your interests at all, but you could consider it if you want to make friends who share those same interests. In the story below, Asha decides to be more open about her interest in reading romance books when she notices Isabella openly reading a book at school.

Asha loves to read romance books, but she is embarrassed about that. Her family is super academic and frowns upon her lack of interest in nonfiction. Asha tries to read literature and social commentary to appear "smart" to her parents, but it is so hard to focus on it. At school, she can't read romance either. She has to read "the classics," which she finds so painfully uninteresting. Eventually, Asha just stopped reading because it wasn't fun anymore.

One day at lunch, Asha spots Isabella reading *The Love Letters of Abelard and Lily* by Laura Creedle and is super impressed that she just puts her interest out there, no matter who sees. "Hey Isabella," Asha says, "is that book any good?" "It's awesome," Isabella responds. "It's about a girl with ADHD and a guy with Asperger's." "No kidding?" says Asha. "That sounds awesome… I kind of want to check that out." In a moment of bravery, Asha says, "If I read that book too, would you want to discuss it sometime?" "Heck yeah," says Isabella. "That would be great. I have some other books I could recommend too if you're interested." "I would love that!" Asha says. Asha decides to give up pretending she doesn't like romance books from that day forward. Eventually, Asha and Isabella create a teen romance book club at their school, and they learn to tune out anyone who makes fun of them. They are enjoying themselves and their interests too much to care.

Are there any interests or dreams that you have been ashamed to share? What would happen if you stopped trying to hide them? Or, if you aren't ready to go public yet, that is okay. You can always take a first step of not hiding these interests from yourself and storing them in a location you'll remember.

_____

_____

_____

_____

Do you have any friends who share interests with you? What interests? How do you feel when you are able to hang out with friends who share some of your treasured interests?

_____

_____

_____

_____

HELP! I DON'T KNOW WHAT MY INTERESTS ARE!

If you're stuck on this question of inspiration and interests, sometimes it can help to think back to what you liked to do before the pressures of being a teen took hold. While some of those previous interests may not appeal to you now, some of them might. Or perhaps some of those interests might take on a new form. For example, if you used to like dressing up dolls, could you enjoy an interest in fashion or thrifting? If you liked to sing in the past, could you download a karaoke app for fun or create some playlists?

What were your interests when you were younger? How can you revive some of those interests in a way that is appealing now?

_____

_____

_____

_____

_____

_____

_____

CHAPTER SUMMARY

CONTENT SUMMARY

 Trying to act like someone else or pretending we have a different life can seem like an appealing idea at first, but may result in challenges in the long term to your mental health and enjoyment of life. Try to practice accepting your life and yourself as you are as often as you can.

 Many girls with ADHD have vocal inner critics who parrot messages they've received from a variety of sources. It can help to become more aware of the sources of these negative messages and start questioning whether your inner critic is giving you true and helpful feedback or not.

 Social expectations for teen girls are extremely high and no one can meet them all. Try to let go of your perfectionistic desire to meet all these expectations and prioritize which activities and pursuits really matter to you.

STRATEGY SUMMARY

 Consider flipping the script on your challenges by seeing them as interesting, and reminding yourself that you are not defined by your challenges.

 Consider labeling or personifying your inner critics. Try being compassionate and accepting for these passengers on your journey, but let them know that you'll be driving the bus.

 Remember to strive for GEMO (good enough, move on), not perfection (it's unattainable anyhow!).

 If changing plans or critical feedback are emotionally hard for you, develop a list of comfort activities you can use.

 Having a list of your values handy can help you develop self-awareness and make good decisions for yourself.

 If you've lost track of your interests, try thinking back to your childhood as a place to start.

CHAPTER 5

LOOK OUT FOR BLIND SPOTS

I would love to assure you that now that you have learned about ADHD, your brain, and yourself, you could drive off into the sunset, happy as a clam, to claim your dream life. That's what would happen in a movie or a book. As you're driving along, managing all the messages and expectations, some of which have wormed there way inside of you as inner critics, you'll have to look out for blind spots. You know how the car's side mirrors say, "Objects in the mirror are closer than they appear"? Just when you thought you were getting a handle on this driving thing, you find there are blind spots in how you are making sense of reality. These common blind spots are called *cognitive distortions*, a term that describes how our brain can take in the world in ways that are inaccurate and unhelpful. Learning how to identify these cognitive distortions and work with them will help you immensely on your journey.

Our brains evolved to categorize reality in simple ways to make it easier to understand. This worked well historically when reality was less complicated. These days, reality is quite complex and many situations are not black or white, but gray. It can be very helpful to start to identify when your brain may be providing you with overly simplistic information about the world. Most often, the simple solution or explanation is overly simplistic.

Black-and-White Thinking

Black-and-white thinking is a common cognitive blind spot that many of our brains engage in. This cognitive distortion involves seeing situations in black or white, or framing decisions as having only two, mutually exclusive options. Isabella shows us an example of how this thinking can distort reality and close off options rather than opening them up.

Isabella is struggling to decide whether she should go to college or move to New York and try to be a successful actress and singer. In her mind, these are two completely separate routes—she would either be a serious performer or she would be a college graduate pursuing a different type of career. Isabella ruminates and ruminates about this, to the point that her friends are getting quite sick of hearing her drama. Finally, Isabella's friend asks a question that Isabella has never thought of: "Is it possible you could do both?" Isabella turns this over in her mind. Maybe she could. What would that look like? Isabella starts looking into college arts programs and reading about how some of her favorite performers got their start. Now she can come up with more ideas about how she might both go to college and keep pursuing her interests.

Black-and-white thinking can be sneaky and hard to identify. We might believe that to be good at something, we must *always* be good at it and *never* struggle (p.s. words like "always" and "never" can be a tip-off that black-and-white thinking is afoot). Asha provides another example of how, if we believe that we can only be good (perfect) or bad at something (imperfect), we might give up on an activity that we're interested in or really enjoy.

Asha loves to sing and many people agree she has great talent, but she has trouble harmonizing and reading music. Asha finds it painful to be quite talented but have this imperfection. Asha decides that she can only be good at music if she is the full, perfect package of a singer who sounds great, can harmonize with others, and has music theory and reading skills. Asha gives up pursuing singing because at times she finds it hard, and her natural talent only gets her so far.

Can you relate to Asha's black-and-white assessment of her talent in singing? Have you ever given up something that you were pretty good at because you weren't perfect at it? When a skill doesn't come easily, how do you cope with that? How would you like to cope with a situation like this in the future?

HOW DO I STOP BLACK-AND-WHITE THINKING?

The first step in reversing any black-and-white thinking or perfectionistic patterns is to become aware of them. Try to have compassion for yourself. These patterns are very common and you've likely been doing it habitually for a while (so have I 😄).

As you start to become more aware of your patterns, become curious about when and where your black-and-white perfectionistic thinking shows up. For example, is it with certain tasks and not others? When certain people are around? Does it occur when you are tired or right before your period?

_____

_____

_____

_____

ACTIVITY 35

Jumping to Conclusions

Many of our brains are quite skilled at jumping to catastrophic and emotion-based conclusions about how a situation will play out in the future. Some people call this cognitive tendency "future-tripping." Our anxious brains can quickly spiral into assumptions about where a particular situation will lead in the future.

In the following example, we see how Jasmine goes from an experience where she has having trouble understanding a math problem to believing she will flunk math, and then even worrying she will be a failure and reinforce negative stereotypes about groups she identifies with.

Jasmine is freaking out. She is really on edge about school and her performance lately. Even though she has been diagnosed with ADHD recently, the process of getting extra support is long and she hasn't gotten all her accommodations in place yet. She is worried about her grades, getting into college, and her future. Jasmine tries so hard to focus on her math homework because she knows studying is the first step in trying to manage these worries and anxieties about negative outcomes. But then she reads the math problem once, and it makes no sense. She takes a deep breath and reads the problem again. It still makes no sense! She grabs her books and runs to the bathroom, where her negative thoughts pour over her. What if she flunks math? What if her teachers think ADHD is just an excuse? What if she just reinforces the awful stereotype of the failing Black student? Jasmine feels terrible, and this leads her to believe that her situation must be terrible. Jasmine can't separate her negative catastrophizing thoughts from the truth of the situation—that one math problem on her homework was very challenging.

Can you relate to Jasmine? Have you ever gone on this type of mental loop spiral after facing a relatively small roadblock or challenge? Can you recall what set off your mental loop spiral?

_____

_____

_____

_____

Can you recall what your inner critic was telling you during the situation you wrote about above? What did your anxious inner critic predict would happen? Looking back, do you think your negative thoughts about the situation were accurate?

_____

_____

_____

_____

When you reflect on your common mental loops, are they more likely to occur when you're feeling down, anxious, calm, or excited? What emotional states make mental spiraling more likely for you?

I'm Spiraling!

When you are spiraling with your thoughts or feelings, it can be helpful to calm your nervous system and de-escalate your stress response. You might considering following one or more of the steps below.

1. Try to distance yourself from the distressing situation by naming it. Therapists often say "name it to tame it" for emotionally charged experiences. Say something like, "My thoughts are spiraling. My emotions are all over the place." These kinds of statements help reinforce that you are not your thoughts or feelings—they are separate from you.

2. Next, try to calm your nervous system by breathing, stretching, or splashing water on your face to further calm your body and slow down your thoughts.

3. Finally, give yourself some encouraging words. You could say to yourself, "You can handle this, you've felt emotions like this before. Feelings come and go, and you are safe. You are not alone; many people have felt feelings like this before. You are okay."

4. Try to practice these strategies not just when you are triggered, but also when you are feeling calm so that they will be easier to remember when you're spiraling!

Of the strategies mentioned above, which do you think might be most helpful for you? What about this particular strategy might be helpful for you?

_____

_____

_____

_____

Negative Filtering

Many of our neurodivergent brains automatically read situations as fairly negative, downplaying the positives of a situation and focusing on the negative. This tendency is described as *negative filtering*. As Rick Hanson describes in his book *Resilient: How to Grow an Unshakable Core of Calm, Strength, and Happiness,* our brains are "Velcro" for negative experiences and "Teflon" for positive experiences. When our brains filter a situation in a negative way, they often inaccurately distort the complexity of a situation. In the example below, Asha sees a mistake she made as extremely negative until her mom steps in and helps view the situation in a different way.

Asha is so upset with herself. She dropped her phone in the toilet *again*. How could she have put her phone in her jeans pocket *again*?! She broods angrily. Her inner critic jumps in, at the ready, leveling insults: "What is wrong with you?!" "When will you learn?" "How can you expect to go to college soon if you are always doing the stupidest things?!" Asha's mom comes in and gives her a hug. "It's okay, sweetie. It's okay." She hugs her and smooths her hair. "You actually haven't dropped your phone in the toilet for a whole year...you are improving! I'm so glad we learned from the last time and got insurance. We'll just get this phone replaced right away; this time we should order a waterproof cover too, right?" "Thanks, Mom," Asha says.

Asha appreciates that her mother can remind her of how she has improved at taking care of her phone, and can help come up with future strategies to safeguard her electronics.

Asha is having a tough executive functioning moment in this example, facing a common challenge that many people with ADHD face. (I have dropped three phones in the toilet so far. How about you?) The next time you get down on yourself for making a mistake, try to step back and see if you are missing any positives about the situation. Often, if we look closely, we can see that we are improving or that the fix to our problem isn't as tricky as we thought. (Now I *always* invest in a shatterproof, waterproof phone case!)

Can you relate to Asha? Have you ever made a mistake like losing or dropping your phone, misplacing your keys, or forgetting your wallet? Have you ever beaten yourself up for these mistakes?

_____

_____

_____

_____

How could you approach these situations in the future to notice some positive or neutral elements? Could you speak to yourself like Asha's mom did and notice how hard you're trying to do better and how you very likely are improving just because of that fact?

_____

_____

_____

_____

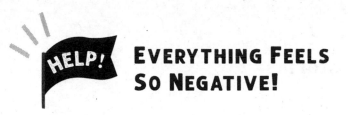

EVERYTHING FEELS
SO NEGATIVE!

A lot of times, because our brains skew to the negative, we don't always notice what is going *right* in our lives. Our culture often encourages us to notice what is wrong and fix it, and we may often see others approaching their lives in this way. However, there is great power in noticing what is going well for us and take time to appreciate that. This can help us counter our brain's automatic tendency to see reality as solely negative. This doesn't mean we should dismiss our negative feelings or expect ourselves to *always* feel grateful; it means instead that we open ourselves to noticing *both* the positive and challenging aspects of our experience. The questions below will help you practice this strategy.

What is going well for you? What do you like about yourself? What do you like about your life?

_____

_____

_____

_____

If you are feeling down, and questions about what is going well or what you like feel overly positive for you today, that's okay. We all feel like that sometimes. Instead, ask yourself, what is going okay for you? What is not so bad about yourself? What is all right or just fine about your life?

_____

_____

_____

_____

Blame Stories

Another way that our brain can distort reality is by either making a situation entirely our fault or by creating a blame story about how the issue is entirely someone else's fault. Blame stories are oriented inward (blaming ourselves) or outward (blaming others). Either way, the most accurate and realistic story is typically more complex than a blame story (McKowen 2022). Many girls with ADHD are more likely to blame themselves than others for the situations they find themselves in, though some of us alternate with blaming others as well. In the case study below, Avery provides an example of a blame story that is getting in the way of her focus at soccer practice.

Avery is having a bad soccer practice. She doesn't want to be there, is having trouble getting started on the boring drills, and feels mad at herself for not being able to make herself focus. Her inner critic keeps poking her, "Get it together, Avery. You've got to work harder and get yourself focused. You've got to let go of this emotional drama." In her irritation, she is snapping at people on the field, which then causes her to self-criticize more because she always tries so hard to be a kind teammate, even if it isn't always obvious to others.

In this example, Avery is focusing on what she is doing, and telling herself she should be doing something different. If Avery could zoom out, she would be able to see that her inability to focus and let go of her internal distractions may not have been entirely under her control. For example, Avery doesn't have control over how the practice is set up or the fact that her ADHD brain struggles in boring situations. If she could zoom out, Avery could understand that on this particular day, the coaches put together a drill-based practice and that other players were also moody and unfocused as a result of the repetition involved. This shows that it's rare for only one person (either you or someone else) to hold all the blame in a situation.

Have you ever blamed yourself for a situation that was likely bigger than you? What was the situation? Draw or describe the situation below.

If you were able to look beyond the blame story in the situation you reflected on, what might you see about the situation? Is there another possible interpretation to this situation, or another way you might approach it?

I'M STUCK IN BLAME STORIES!

If your brain starts to spin a lot of blame stories, you are not alone. The trick is to start noticing them and then, when you have some time, to slow down and reflect on the story your brain is telling you. The blame story may be about someone else, or it may be about yourself. Either way, it's likely leaving out some important complexity to the situation. To become more aware of your blame stories, you might select one of the following strategies:

★ Discuss the issue with a therapist or coach.

★ Journal on your own or periodically use the journaling prompts above to reflect when you suspect a blame story might have occurred for you.

★ Find a friend who has similar challenges who could be a sounding board. If you are in an ADHD or EF support group, is there someone there you can partner with to be sounding boards for each other, checking whether your interpretation of life events makes sense?

Mind Reading

Sometimes we assume that we can read other people's thoughts and motives from their words or actions. However, this can also be a distortion. For example, because many of us are sensitive, we can often read into others' behavior cues as being about us. For example, Avery often interprets others' actions as rejections of her.

Avery has a big and growing crush on Zane, captain of the boys' soccer team. Avery suspects that because she is a tomboy, and questions her gender identity, that she is probably not Zane's type. Zane usually dates cheerleader types. However, Avery can't stop thinking about Zane, so she decides to test the waters by asking Zane if he is available to practice soccer with her this weekend. She is going to pretend that she needs help with learning how to juggle because she has heard that guys love it when girls act like they are not good at something. Avery is so nervous...she finally sees Zane out of the corner of her eye. He kind of looks like he is rushing, but Avery just has to do this and get it over with and move on. She charges toward him and blurts out her question. "Hi, Zane. Do you want to help me learn how to juggle this weekend?" "Hi, Avery, sorry, I gotta go. See you around later." He rushes off. Avery is devastated and feels like she has just been blown off and rejected. She feels super embarrassed and vows she will never ask Zane out again.

The backstory to this situation was that Zane was surprised by Avery and had been lost in his own thoughts. He didn't even really hear Avery's question, especially since Avery's delivery was so fast. More than any sort of rejection, miscommunication shaped this interaction between Avery and Zane.

Can you relate to Avery's situation? Have you ever interpreted a situation as a rejection that may have actually been a miscommunication?

_____

_____

_____

_____

_____

_____

How would you advise Avery to handle her feelings of rejection, both in this particular situation and in an ongoing way in her life?

_____

_____

_____

_____

_____

HELP! I THINK I'VE BEEN REJECTED!

Keep your eye out for when you feel you've been rejected. This can be a sign that you might be in cognitive distortion and emotional sensitivity territory. People with ADHD can often interpret another person's changes in tone and distractibility as intentional messages of rejection. When you feel you've been rejected, try to slow down and ask yourself some questions to see whether you are really interpreting the situation correctly. What other interpretations of the situation might exist? If you don't like to reflect in your head or in writing, consider talking to a trusted friend to get their feedback and whether they think you've correctly assessed the situation.

Just like others shouldn't interpret our ADHD challenges as meaning that we're lazy, disrespectful, or don't care, we should try to figure out whether we are reading rejection into the behaviors of others that they don't intend. It has been helpful for me to realize that some people have trouble sensing whether their tone sounds frustrated or annoyed. Some people say things without thinking, and this has hurt my feelings. I remind myself that they may not know what kind of things hurt my feelings and that they may not know that I'm so sensitive. Some people also have difficulty with social skills and empathy. I try to have compassion for these folks and take their behavior with a large grain of salt. Maybe they're struggling with empathy, intentional words, and social awareness just like I struggle with cleaning my room and adapting to changes in plans.

Can you think of anyone you know who may seem to be rejecting of others but may, in reality, be struggling with social skills, communication, and empathy? What strengths and challenges might this person have? How can you try to empathize with them?

_____

_____

_____

_____

CHAPTER SUMMARY

CONTENT SUMMARY

In the chart below, review the cognitive distortion blind spots that people with ADHD often have. Which of the following have you experienced most? In the rating column, mark "O" for often, "S" for sometimes, and "N" for never. You'll also find a copy of this chart at the website for this book: http://www.newharbinger.com/52809. You can come back to this chart over time as you gain self-awareness and are better able to notice your behavior and symptoms.

COGNITIVE DISTORTION BLIND SPOTS		
COGNITIVE DISTORTION	**DEFINITION**	**O, S, OR N**
Black-and-white thinking	Seeing things in black or white, as having only two options or choices. For example, "I can do this or that. There are no other options."	
Jumping to conclusions	Generalizing one experience to all other, similar experiences. For example, "I didn't get into the first college I applied to. I will never get into college."	
Negative filtering	Seeing very few or no positives in a situation.	
Blame stories	Blaming the entire context of a situation on yourself or something else. For example, "This is all your fault!"	
Mind reading	Coming to an extreme conclusion because of a small slice of a social interaction. For example, "She isn't paying any attention to me...she hates me!"	

STRATEGY SUMMARY

★ Try to observe your common thinking patterns and emotional reactions, and "name them to tame them."

★ When you're upset, try to ask yourself if your brain is trying to convince you that a small problem is much more impactful than it really is.

★ Try to frequently ask questions about what you might be missing or what else might be going on. What positive or a-okay elements might you be missing in a given situation? Ask questions about what you are missing and what else might be going on.

★ If you notice a blame story, congrats! How might the situation be bigger than blame?

★ Notice if you're assuming others' intentions from their tone or actions. Could you ask them about their intent or use a friend as a sounding board if it's too intimidating to talk to the person directly?

CHAPTER 6

GUIDEPOSTS FOR THE JOURNEY

ere we are at the final chapter. We've journeyed through ADHD definitions and discussions of history to get to where we are today. We've learned about our brains, ourselves, and the blind spots that often shape our interpretation of events. Thinking about where we're going takes a lot of the same skills that were required along the journey. We need to feel a range of feelings, acknowledge complexity, and be flexible. We must find a balance between trying to manage our challenges and leaning into our strengths. The horizon is a fitting metaphor for where we are heading because it's different at different times of day, but there are patterns if we continue our efforts to observe and understand.

There are some key patterns of activities and mindsets that will benefit your ADHD, and these are fitting for a closing chapter. Even as you may get off track and take detours (sometimes these turn out to be the best parts!), the guideposts in this chapter can help ground you. The goal is not to arrive at the horizon, because—spoiler alert!—we never really will. We will never arrive, never be perfect—but that is not the point. The point is to show up for the journey with as much grace and acceptance as we can. When you feel lost or confused (and you will, we all do), you can come back to the ideas in this chapter to hopefully connect with yourself, remember what is important to you, and keep moving forward.

ACTIVITY 39

Revise Definitions of Failure and Success

hat is failure? What is success? How do you define it? Growing up, I labeled all kinds of things with the f-word (failure). The idea that you learn from failure didn't make sense to me, especially because I was emotionally triggered by my failures and the reasonable and reflective part of my brain went offline. All I learned from many experiences was "that sucked, I suck. I am a failure." I labeled all my ADHD weaknesses as failures too. What was I defining as success? I was defining it as the opposite of failure: perfection. The trouble with this was that I could never reach this because the bar was too high. If I was trying to change a habit brushing my teeth two times a day, I never noticed the days I succeeded. I only noticed the days I didn't, labeling all the other days as failures because I hadn't done it every day.

What other story could I have told about my attempts at brushing my teeth twice a day? Could I tell a story of success because I was stepping up to the plate again and again? Could I count all the days I did my new habit as progress, as moving in the direction of success?

_____

_____

_____

_____

Think of a "failure" you had. Can you tell a new story that is more compassionate and empowering for you?

_____

_____

_____

_____

Have there been any successes you didn't give yourself credit for because they weren't perfect or didn't remain successful each and every day forever? Can you go back and give yourself credit for trying, showing up, and how much you cared?

_____

_____

_____

_____

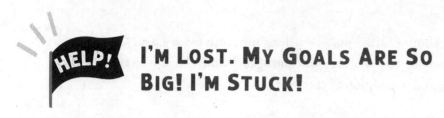

HELP! I'm Lost. My Goals Are So Big! I'm Stuck!

Sometimes when we feel lost, everything seems so big, heavy, and hard. Changing our habits feels hard, working on our mental health feels hard, reaching out to others feels hard. In that moment, try to think of just taking one super small step. Bonus points for picking a step so small it is almost funny (e.g., brushing one tooth or doing one push-up à la Stephen Guise's 2013 book *Mini Habits*).

What are some possible small steps that would feel doable and would move you in the direction of your current goals?

Goals: _____

Brainstorm small steps for these goals:

_____

_____

_____

_____

Which steps might be good first steps? Which steps could be good later steps?

_____

_____

_____

_____

Creativity

Being creative is a superpower of ours. In fact, having a creative outlet might just save your life. ADHDers are super creative and this is part of why we see so many famous ADHDers doing some really cool stuff, like starting businesses, writing books, singing, dancing, and performing! Famous ADHDers include Jennifer Lopez, Emma Watson, and Paris Hilton, just to name a few. Sometimes our ADHD challenges show up to the party too, at times getting in the way of our progress. Try to stick with your creativity, even if you struggle at times. Dr. Hallowell and Dr. Ratey (2021) encourage all people with ADHD to find a creative outlet that meets their need for brain stimulation something productive rather than relying on unhealthy or addictive behaviors to cope.

As Hallowell and Ratey (2021) mention, many of us have an itch for *more* that we want to scratch. We want life to be *more* than just ordinary. This energy and drive is a great strength, but it can cause us trouble if we don't know how to harness it in a creative outlet. Having a creative outlet can be a place to direct this energy, even if we engage in creativity just for ourselves, and fostering this creative outlet outside of school or work can keep us going. It's not that we will necessarily make our creative outlet our course of study or our job, but instead, we will always have this outlet for our strengths and interests.

In general, ADHDers are often great at making creative connections and also brainstorming ideas. This can show up in lots of areas, not just the creative arts. ADHDers are often wonderful at problem-solving all sorts of things, including people problems, design problems, and organizational problems. We think of unique ideas (many, many ideas!) and we can often see innovative connections between ideas and concepts. However, we often struggle to narrow down those ideas (prioritization) and stay on track with our creative projects.

Do you relate to any of the ADHD creative strengths described above? Do you have *lots* of ideas? About what topics? In which areas of your life do they show up?

_____

_____

_____

_____

Do you make connections that others don't, either between different subjects or different ideas? Have you been told you take conversations to another level of insight? Can you describe an experience when someone noticed your creative, idea-generating insights?

_____

_____

_____

_____

_____

Do you have a creative outlet or outlets? What are they?

_____

_____

_____

_____

_____

Do you engage in your creative outlet as much as you would like? If not, how might you work it into your life a little more?

_____

_____

_____

_____

_____

HELP! MY ADHD IS GETTING IN THE WAY OF MY CREATIVE OUTLET!

If your creativity is troubled by some ADHD challenges, try to use that creativity to brainstorm ways to become unstuck or to think of supportive individuals or resources you could tap into to help with your challenges. I've listed a few possible strategies below if you are having trouble making progress with your creative outlet.

Place a star next to the strategies you might consider trying in the list below:

_____ Take a perspective outside yourself and pretend you are a friend giving yourself advice about strategies you might try to make creative progress. Write down all the possible solutions "your friend" might come up with. After listing all your ideas, circle the one to three best ideas for making progress.

_____ Ask a friend or family member to listen to all your ideas about your progress and help you narrow them down to a top idea or two. You might consider chatting with them about the pros and cons of one idea versus another.

_____ Ask a friend or family member to be an accountability buddy who sits with you while you work or checks in with you about your progress.

_____ Find accountability for your creative outlet by taking a class or joining a group or club. Many of us are more likely to work on our creative project if we have to show it off at a particular time with other people.

Which of the above strategies did you mark as ones you might try to get your creative outlet going? What made you choose those strategies?

_____

_____

_____

_____

_____

What is a first step you could take to get some support for developing your creativity?

_____

_____

_____

_____

ACTIVITY 41

Connection and Belonging

Real belonging comes when you no longer have to hide key parts of yourself from others. If connection is a goal of yours, you can work on finding true belonging by becoming more aware of the masks that you commonly put on. This reflection will help you become aware of when you're not being authentic and true to yourself. The more you can show up as your authentic self, the more you'll be able to find the communities and spaces where you truly belong.

If you have trouble making "true" friends or don't even know what that would look like, you are not alone. Many girls with ADHD have trouble making friends or finding solid friendships. First, there is the fact that a lot of our ADHD symptoms can make it hard to be attentive in social relationships. Our distractibility can make it hard for us to focus on what people are saying, we may interrupt others due to our impulsivity, or we may have difficulty following through on social engagements. For me, I always had trouble with low social battery stamina unless I was with a friend who I really connected with and felt comfortable around. The research shows that ADHD girls who have one friend like this are much less likely to experience challenges and risky behavior in their teen years (Nadeau, Littman, and Quinn 2016).

If you do not have a true, high-quality friendships this time, friend, that is okay and you are not alone in that. It can be hard to find places where we can be ourselves and take off our masks. If we haven't found people like this around us, we may not know where to start looking. For many folks with ADHD, great places to start looking for friends can be ADHD support groups or groups of people who share your interests. A lot of times we can socialize quite well around others who face similar ADHD challenges or strengths and/or have similar interests to us. In working with many clients, I have seen the magic of relating to others with similar ADHD challenges. In the example below, Asha and Isabella found a connection like this.

Asha signed up to be a peer tutor because she wanted to put it on her college applications. She was supposed to tutor someone named Isabella, a junior, but this person hasn't showed. Asha sighs; she has places to be and things to do. Then Isabella comes barreling in, finally. Asha looks her over, noticing she is well put together and made up. In contrast, Asha is makeup free, hair pulled up in a messy bun. Isabella plops her stuff down and says, "So sorry! ADHD strikes again with the time blindness." Asha laughs, surprised that this girl who looks so pretty and popular could have ADHD. "ADHD does make things zesty, doesn't it?" Asha commiserates. "You have ADHD, too?" Isabella asks. "But you're clearly so smart and on top of things." Asha laughs again. "Ask me how many times I've dropped my phone in the toilet." Isabella's eyes swell. "How many times?!" Asha smiles. "Three!" "OMG!" Isabella starts snort laughing. "I guess having issues with time isn't so bad in that case..." "Yeah," says Asha, "if your phone stays dry and urine free, you should count yourself lucky." Just like that, Asha and Isabella became fast friends, study partners, and accountability buddies for the rest of the year.

Do you have any friendships where you can mutually support each other about similar challenges that you face? Describe a person you can commiserate with below. Do you have any friends or contacts with ADHD? Have you ever tried reaching out to see if you might connect?

HELP! I'M NOT SURE IF I HAVE TRUE FRIENDSHIPS!

Sometimes our friends are just whoever is around us and we don't always feel like we have much control over who our friends are. Even if you don't feel like you have a lot of choice, it can help to reflect on what you might enjoy in future friendships or how you might make current friendships more satisfying. You are definitely not alone if friendships are tricky for you or you find yourself stumped by them at times. The questions below will help you get started on reflecting about what kind of friends you have and want, and where you might be able to find people who share your interests.

Describe a friend you have; it could be your closest friend or a friend who you spend the most time with. What do you like about this friend? What do you enjoy doing with this friend? Is there anything about this friendship you would like to change to make it more satisfying for you?

_____

_____

_____

_____

What are you looking for in your friendships? Do you feel satisfied in your current friendships?

What are your ideal activities to do with friends? (For me, I enjoy short walks, coffee dates, movies, and going to exercise classes. 😊)

_____

_____

_____

_____

Stand Up for Yourself with Healthy Boundaries

Setting boundaries or limits is an essential skill as we learn more about ourselves and how to advocate for our needs. However, it is often not easy and we may not have been shown how to do this effectively. For those getting started, Veronica Valli (2022) offers a helpful refrain to aid us in how to set boundaries: *Say what you mean, mean what you say, don't say it mean.*

SAY WHAT YOU MEAN—This means that you say things that are generally truthful and authentic and that you get to the point without excessive explanation. If you are going to say no to something, say no and don't feel you need to keep explaining. You can make a boundary confusing to someone else if you provide unnecessary detail or justification for it. According to Valli's definition, masking often or being inauthentic would not meet the criteria of "say what you mean."

MEAN WHAT YOU SAY—This means that you say yes when you plan to follow through on things and no when you don't plan to follow through or you don't really want to do the thing. This sounds easy, but many of us find this hard due to our challenges with overcommitting and people pleasing. To do this well, you need a lot of self-awareness about what commitments serve you and how much you can manage on your plate at one time.

DON'T SAY IT MEAN—This can be hard to do, especially when we haven't set firm boundaries with someone in the past. Especially when we are first setting boundaries with people we haven't set boundaries with before, they may push back or try to negotiate with us. Our goal is to reiterate the boundary in a kind and compassionate way, without giving in or adding unnecessary explanation. We should also be prepared that we may experience "afterburn" when we set a boundary, meaning that we may experience anxiety about doing something we haven't done before and we're not sure how the other person will take it. Over time, we will experience less afterburn and others will test us less as we teach them that we will stick to our boundaries. For example, Jasmine was having trouble maintaining her boundaries. Read the example below and reflect on which aspects of boundary-setting Jasmine was having trouble with.

> Jasmine's brother is always asking for things—her time, attention, allowance—and she often gives in just so he will leave her alone. Jasmine's therapist mentioned this issue, so Jasmine is trying to change her approach with her brother. Today, when Jasmine's brother asked for some money, Jasmine said no. Jasmine's brother was surprised by Jasmine's response and started yelling that she was the worst sister ever. Jasmine eventually couldn't stand the noise and gave her brother the money.

What advice would you give to Jasmine about setting boundaries with her brother?

_____

_____

_____

_____

_____

Why do you think Jasmine backs down with her brother? What is she afraid of? How could you encourage Jasmine to take a small step toward improvement?

_____

_____

_____

_____

_____

What benefits would Jasmine experience if she followed through on boundary setting? When do you imagine she would start experiencing those benefits?

_____

_____

_____

_____

_____

HELP! I SUCK AT BOUNDARIES!

If you feel this way, you are definitely not alone. Many of us weren't taught these skills early on. In all honesty, I am still working on these skills as a middle-aged woman. Sometimes I get down on myself for how hard this is for me. I am often uncomfortable with conflict or displeasing others. However, I also try to have compassion for myself and notice the progress I'm making. I know that I will likely always be working on this skill, and that's okay. I try to forgive and learn from every mistake, and celebrate every super small step in the right direction. Even if you take no action after reading this activity, you are still doing something. You are still moving in the right direction of knowing yourself, advocating for yourself and, one day, setting the boundaries and limits that can help you thrive.

Setting boundaries is a complex, multistep process that can take a long time to master. Even if you aren't ready to stand up for yourself with others yet, that's okay. Learning about yourself and your needs is a great first step. As you do the work of learning about yourself, you will gain increased confidence and self-awareness, which will help you set boundaries with others. All this learning and self-awareness work that you do counts and will contribute to your ongoing ability to set boundaries and get your needs met in the future.

How, if at all, have you increased your self-awareness as you've completed this workbook? What needs, self-acceptance, and awareness have you discovered?

_____

_____

_____

_____

_____

_____

_____

Reflect on a time you stood up yourself, if you've ever done so. What did this look like? How did it feel? If you've never done this (that's okay), reflect instead on a time you saw someone else stand up for you or another person. How did they do it?

_____

_____

_____

_____

_____

_____

_____

_____

Are there people in your life with whom you'd like to have better boundaries? What would you like to change? Based on your current goals and priorities, do you plan to work on these goals sooner or later? (It's okay to say "later" if your plate is full and you have other, more important or pressing things to work on.)

_____

_____

_____

_____

_____

_____

_____

_____

CHAPTER SUMMARY

CONTENT SUMMARY

✓ Notice when you first label an experience as a "failure" or a "success," and start to get curious. Try to revise your definitions to make them realistic, compassionate, and ADHD-friendly for your brain.

✓ Fostering a creative outlet uses ADHD strengths and helps meet our needs for more brain stimulation in a healthy way. 😊

✓ It's easier to connect and belong with others when we find places where we can be ourselves, warts and all. Finding true belonging and connection won't happen overnight, but it is a great long-term thing to strive for.

✓ Working on setting boundaries can support you in being authentic, getting your needs met, and having satisfying relationships. These skills can take time to acquire, but are often well worth the long-term effort.

STRATEGY SUMMARY

★ When you feel stuck, try to take a tiny, small step toward your goal. A tiny step can often get us started. Even if it doesn't get you a long distance, you can still celebrate a tiny step!

★ If your ADHD symptoms are getting in the way of engaging with your creative outlet, consider brainstorming how to get started, finding an accountability buddy or sounding board, or taking a class.

★ If you don't have true friends you can be yourself with yet, try finding them in your interest areas, or seek out others who may have ADHD or similar challenges with whom you can commiserate.

★ To start practicing improving your boundaries, remember: *say what you mean, mean what you say,* and *don't say it mean.* If you make a mistake, you can try again another time. Many of us are still working on this!

CATHERINE'S SHORT LIST OF FAVORITE RESOURCES

LEARNING MORE ABOUT YOUR STRENGTHS

VIA Character Strengths Survey

DECISION-MAKING SUPPORT

Spinnerwheel.com

Spin the Wheel App

FICTION WRITERS WHO WRITE ABOUT TEEN CHARACTERS WITH ADHD

Mazey Eddings

Laura Creedle

YOUTUBE CHANNELS

How to ADHD

The Holderness Family

ADHD COMICS

Dani Donovan

TOOLS TO BOOST EXECUTIVE FUNCTION

Tile App (helps with finding keys, phone, and other important items!)

Tapping Solution App (an active form of meditation that helps with emotional control and mental flexibility)

Day One Journal App (helps with organizing your photos, voice memos, and other information you collect into notebooks)

BOOKS ABOUT EXECUTIVE FUNCTION (WITH ASSESSMENTS!)

Smart but Scattered for Teens by Richard Guare, Peggy Dawson, and Colin Guare

The Executive Functioning Workbook for Teens by Sharon Hansen

ACKNOWLEDGMENTS

I would like to thank many people who supported the work of writing this book. First and foremost, I would like to thank myself. This was a journey that required a lot of persistence, and it also required confronting a lot of common ADHD internal demons, such as perfectionism, procrastination, self-sabotage, and imposter syndrome. I am proud of myself for continuing on with the process in spite of these mental and emotional challenges that made numerous appearances along the way.

That being said, this process was so much easier than it could have been. I am grateful for the support of Elizabeth Hollis Hansen, who encouraged me through the proposal, contract, and early book development process. I greatly appreciate how friendly this process was for my ADHD brain. I appreciate all the expertise and templates and feedback provided by New Harbinger and my editors. I thrive with this kind of structure, deadlines, and encouragement.

Finally, I would like to thank all of the people who supported me, including my husband, Glenn Mutti-Driscoll; my wonderful friend, Sara Nagel, who let me use her house for a writing retreat; and my kids and parents, for always cheering me on. I also appreciate the many friends who offered support and encouragement along the way as I juggled the ups and downs of writing my first book as well as parenting, work, and grad school. Special shout out to Fran, Sprout, Emily, Jo, Kathryn G., Kathryn F., Jovana, Lesley, Elise, and the lovely Sober Mom Squad community. *Thank you.*

REFERENCES

Beck, M. 2021. *The Way of Integrity: Finding the Path to Your True Self*. London: Piatkus.

Katie, B., with S. Michell. 2021. *Loving What Is: Four Questions That Can Change Your Life*. Rev. ed. New York: Harmony Books.

Cameron, J. 2016. *The Artist's Way: A Spiritual Path to Higher Creativity*, 25th ann. ed. London: Souvenir Press.

David, S. 2016. *Emotional Agility: Get Unstuck, Embrace Change, and Thrive in Work and Life*. New York: Penguin Life Books.

Dodson, W. 2022. "3 Defining Features of ADHD That Everyone Overlooks." *ADDitude Magazine*. https://www.additudemag.com/symptoms-of-add-hyperarousal-rejection-sensitivity.

Guare, D., P. Dawson, and C. Guare. 2013. *Smart but Scattered Teens: The "Executive Skills" Program for Helping Teens Reach Their Potential*. New York: Guilford Press.

Gilbert, E. 2015. *Big Magic: Creative Living Beyond Fear*. New York: Riverhead Books.

Guise, S. 2013. *Mini Habits: Smaller Habits, Bigger Results*. CreateSpace Independent Publishing Platform.

Hallowell, E. M. 2023. "Reframing ADHD." *The Hallowell ADHD Centers*. https://drhallowell.com/2019/10/03/reframing-adhd.

Hallowell, E. M., and J. J. Ratey. 2021. *ADHD 2.0: New Science and Essential Strategies for Thriving with Distraction—from Childhood Through Adulthood*. New York: Ballantine Books.

Hanson, R., with F. Hanson. 2018. *Resilient: How to Grow an Unshakable Core of Calm, Strength, and Happiness*. New York: Harmony Books.

McCabe, J. 2016. "ADHD in Girls: How to Recognize the Symptoms." *How to ADHD* (YouTube), April 13. https://www.youtube.com/watch?v=dmeE3qTJRUw.

———. 2021. "ADHD in Women." *How to ADHD* (YouTube), August 31. https://www.youtube.com/watch?v=EMpt40zNK-w.

McKowen, L. 2023. *Push Off from Here: Nine Essential Truths to Get You Through Sobriety (and Everything Else)*. New York: Ballantine Books.

Nadeau, K. G., E. B. Littman, and P. O. Quinn. 2016. *Understanding Girls with ADHD: How They Feel and Why They Do What They Do*. Santa Fe, NM: Advantage Books.

Price, D. 2021. *Laziness Does Not Exist: A Defense of the Exhausted, Exploited, and Overworked*. New York: Atria Books.

Solden, S., and M. Frank. 2019. *A Radical Guide for Women with ADHD: Embrace Neurodiversity, Live Boldly, and Break Through Barriers*. Oakland, CA: New Harbinger Publications.

Taylor-Klaus, E., and D. Dempster. 2016. *Parenting ADHD Now: Easy Intervention Strategies to Empower Kids with ADHD*. Berkeley, CA: Althea Press.

Valli, V. 2022. *Soberful: Uncover a Sustainable, Fulfilling Life Free of Alcohol*. Boulder, CO: Sounds True.

CATHERINE J. MUTTI-DRISCOLL, PHD, loves to learn, and has a variety of degrees and certifications. Highlights include Catherine's PhD in education from the University of Washington, and her coach training from the International ADHD Coach Training Center and Impact Parents. Catherine is currently at Walden University studying to become a licensed mental health counselor.

Writing a book has been a lifelong dream of Catherine's. When she is not working, studying, or writing, she enjoys hanging out with her neurodivergent family (one spouse and two sons!), drinking coffee with friends, dancing to Taylor Swift, and reading contemporary romances. Catherine lives in Seattle, WA.

Foreword writer **EDWARD M. HALLOWELL, MD,** is a child and adult psychiatrist, leading authority in the field of ADHD, *New York Times* bestselling author, and world-renowned speaker. He is founder of The Hallowell Centers for Cognitive and Emotional Health in Boston MetroWest; New York, NY; San Francisco, CA; and Seattle, WA.